THE HOPE AND LIFE PRESS CHRISTIANITY SERIES

Teachings of the Catholic Church

HOPE AND LIFE PRESS

First published in 2018 by
HOPE AND LIFE PRESS

The Hope and Life Press Christianity Series

ISBN 978-17238-3-099-0 paperback edition.

Copyright © 2018 Hope and Life Press – All rights reserved.

Published by
HOPE AND LIFE PRESS

All rights reserved. No part of this work may be reproduced, stored in a retrieval system, or submitted in any form or by any means, electronic, mechanical, photocopying, recording or otherwise, without the prior written permission of the publisher. This book may not be lent, resold, hired out or otherwise disposed of by way of trade in any form of binding or cover other than that in which it is published, without the prior written consent of the publishers.

Printed in the United States of America.

CONTENTS

BOOK 1: Can 'Just War' Exist?	5
BOOK 2: Is Islam a Religion?	17
BOOK 3: Migrants and Refugees in Catholic Social Doctrine	35
BOOK 4: Is the Death Penalty Just?	61
BOOK 5: What is the Magisterium of the Catholic Church?	75
BOOK 6: The Divine Heart of God the Father in Scripture	81

BOOK I

CAN 'JUST WAR' EXIST?

I desire mercy not sacrifice (Hos 6:6, Mt 9:13).

Just War According to the Scholastics

Saint Augustine

Formal 'just war' doctrine in Western Christianity is thought to have commenced with Saint Augustine. This was based on the following passage written by the Apostle Paul in his *Letter to the Romans:*

> *For the one in authority is God's servant for your good. But if you do wrong, be afraid, for rulers do not bear the sword for no reason. They are God's servants, agents of wrath to bring punishment on the wrongdoer (13:4).*

Augustine, in his *Contra Faustum Manichaeum,* argued that Christians did not need to feel ashamed of protecting peace and punishing wickedness when mandated to do so by a government. However, he asserted that this argument was personal and philosophical: "What is here required is not a bodily action, but an inward disposition." In the meantime, in his work *The City of God,* Augustine elaborated:

> *They who have waged war in obedience to the divine command, or in conformity with His laws, have represented in their persons the public justice or the wisdom of government, and in this capacity have put to death wicked men; such persons have by no means violated the commandment 'Thou shalt not kill'. . . . the wise man will wage Just Wars. As if he would not all the rather lament the necessity of just wars, if he remembers that he is a man; for if they were not just he would not wage them, and would therefore be delivered from all wars.*

Saint Thomas Aquinas

In the *Summa Theologica* written 900 years later, Saint Thomas Aquinas revised Augustine's stance by formulating three criteria that were *all* required to be met in order for a war to be considered 'just.' These criteria were that:
1. The war had to be declared and waged by a legitimate authority (e.g., the state);
2. The cause for war had to be *both* just and good (e.g., to restore something that had been lost), rather than carried out for self-gain or power; and
3. The right intent for the war needed to underlie the decision to go to war.

Specifically, according to Thomas:

In order for a war to be just, three things are necessary. First, the authority of the sovereign by whose command the war is to be waged. For it is not the business of a private individual to declare war, because he can seek for redress of his rights from the tribunal of his superior. Moreover, it is not the business of a private individual to summon together the people, which has to be done in wartime. And as the care of the commonweal is committed to those who are in authority, it is their business to watch over the commonweal of the city, kingdom or province subject to them. And just as it is lawful for them to have recourse to the sword in defending that commonweal against internal disturbances, when they punish evil-doers, according to the words of the Apostle (Romans 13:4): "He beareth not the sword in vain: for he is God's minister, an avenger to execute wrath upon him that doth evil;" so too, it is their business to have recourse to the sword of war in defending the commonweal against external enemies. Hence it is said to those who are in authority (Ps 81:4): "Rescue the poor: and deliver the needy out of the hand of the sinner;" and for this reason Augustine says (Contra Faust. xxii, 75): "The natural order conducive to peace among mortals demands that the power to declare and counsel war should be in the hands of those who hold the supreme authority."

Secondly, a just cause is required, namely that those who are attacked, should be attacked because they deserve it on account of some fault. Wherefore Augustine says (QQ. in Hept., qu. x, super Jos.): "A just war is wont to be described as one that avenges wrongs, when a nation or state has to be punished, for refusing to make amends for the wrongs inflicted by its subjects, or to restore what it has seized unjustly."

Thirdly, it is necessary that the belligerents should have a rightful intention so that they intend the advancement of good or the avoidance of evil. Hence Augustine says (Can. Apud. Caus. xxiii, qu. 1): "True religion looks upon as peaceful those wars that are waged not for motives of aggrandizement or cruelty, but with the object of securing peace, of punishing evil-doers, and of uplifting the good." For it may happen that the war is declared by the legitimate authority and for a just cause, and yet be rendered unlawful through a wicked intention. Hence Augustine says (Contra Faust. xxii, 74): "The passion for inflicting harm, the cruel thirst for vengeance, an unpacific and relentless spirit, the fever of revolt, the lust of power and such like things, all these are rightly condemned in war" (Question 40: War).

Thus, the three criteria set forth by Thomas were elaborated into the following seven sub-criteria that *all* needed to be met for a 'just war' to be in effect:
1. It had to be carried out as a last resort;
2. This could only be done by a legitimate authority;
3. The war to be carried out for a truly just cause (i.e., not just *any* cause);
4. There had to be a significant probability of success as a result of the proposed war;
5. The intent underlying the decision to go to war had to be 'right' (i.e., not in revenge for perceived or actual wrongs);
6. The degree of force used could never be more than what was needed to attain success (i.e., proportionality); and
7. Civilians could never be the primary target of the war.

Just War in Patristics

No just war doctrine exists in most of the writings of the Greek Fathers. Even in the case of circumstances often considered to be 'unavoidable,' these Fathers of the Church repeatedly maintained that war was the lesser of greater evils, but evil nonetheless. Saint Athanasius, however, declared that:

*Although one is not supposed to kill, the killing of the enemy in time of war is both a lawful and praiseworthy thing. This is why we consider individuals who have distinguished themselves in war as being worthy of great honors, and indeed public monuments are set up to celebrate their achievements. It is evident, therefore, that at one particular time, and under one set of circumstances, an act is not permissible, but when time and circumstances are right, it is both allowed and condoned (*Letter to Amun*).*

And Saint Basil the Great maintained that:

*Our Fathers did not consider the killings committed in the course of wars to be classifiable as murders at all, on the score, it seems to me, of allowing a pardon to men fighting in defense of sobriety and piety. Perhaps, though, it might be advisable to refuse them communion for three years, on the ground that they are not clean-handed (*Canon 13*).*

Just War Doctrine in Modern Times

The Catechism of the Catholic Church

In *The Catechism of the Catholic Church* (2003), four conditions have been listed as necessary for any war to be considered morally legitimate. These conditions are that:

1. *The damage inflicted by the aggressor on the nation or community of nations must be lasting, grave, and certain;*
2. *All other means of putting an end to it must have been shown to be impractical or ineffective;*

3. *There must be serious prospects of success; and*
4. *The use of arms must not produce evils and disorders graver than the evil to be eliminated. The power of modern means of destruction weighs very heavily in evaluating this condition.*

The Compendium of the Social Doctrine of the Church

In the meantime, at the instigation of Saint John Paul II, the Pontifical Council of Justice and Peace (2004) elaborated on the 'just war' doctrine in its *Compendium of the Social Doctrine of the Church*:

If this responsibility justifies the possession of sufficient means to exercise this right to defence, States still have the obligation to do everything possible "to ensure that the conditions of peace exist, not only within their own territory but throughout the world." It is important to remember that "it is one thing to wage a war of self-defence; it is quite another to seek to impose domination on another nation. The possession of war potential does not justify the use of force for political or military objectives. Nor does the mere fact that war has unfortunately broken out mean that all is fair between the warring parties." The Charter of the United Nations intends to preserve future generations from war with a prohibition against force to resolve disputes between States. Like most philosophy, it permits legitimate defence and measures to maintain peace. In every case, the Charter requires that self-defence must respect the traditional limits of necessity and proportionality. Therefore, engaging in a preventive war without clear proof that an attack is imminent cannot fail to raise serious moral and juridical questions. International legitimacy for the use of armed force, on the basis of rigorous assessment and with well-founded motivations, can only be given by the decision of a competent body that identifies specific situations as threats to peace and authorizes an intrusion into the sphere of autonomy usually reserved to a State.

And they shall beat their swords into plowshares, and their spears into pruning-hooks: nation shall not lift up sword against nation, neither shall they learn war any more (Is 2:4).

Saint John XXIII and Subsequent Popes

Saint John XXIII fearlessly declared that it was "contrary to reason to consider war as a suitable way to restore rights." He added:

> *There is a common belief that under modern conditions peace cannot be assured except on the basis of an equal balance of armaments and that this factor is the probable cause of this stockpiling of armaments. Thus, if one country increases its military strength, others are immediately roused by a competitive spirit to augment their own supply of armaments. And if one country is equipped with atomic weapons, others consider themselves justified in producing such weapons themselves, equal in destructive force . . . Hence justice, right reason, and the recognition of man's dignity cry out insistently for a cessation to the arms race. The stock-piles of armaments which have been built up in various countries must be reduced all round and simultaneously by the parties concerned. Nuclear weapons must be banned. A general agreement must be reached on a suitable disarmament program, with an effective system of mutual control. In the words of Pope Pius XII: "The calamity of a world war, with the economic and social ruin and the moral excesses and dissolution that accompany it, must not on any account be permitted to engulf the human race for a third time."*
>
> *Everyone, however, must realize that, unless this process of disarmament be thoroughgoing and complete, and reach men's very souls, it is impossible to stop the arms race, or to reduce armaments, or—and this is the main thing—ultimately to abolish them entirely. Everyone must sincerely co-operate in the effort to banish fear and the anxious expectation of war from men's minds. But this requires that the fundamental principles upon which peace is based in today's world be replaced by an altogether different one, namely, the realization that true and lasting peace among nations cannot consist in the possession of an equal supply of armaments but only in mutual trust. And We are confident that this can be achieved, for it is a thing which not only is dictated by common sense, but is in itself most desirable and most fruitful of good . . .*

Men nowadays are becoming more and more convinced that any disputes which may arise between nations must be resolved by negotiation and agreement, and not by recourse to arms. We acknowledge that this conviction owes its origin chiefly to the terrifying destructive force of modern weapons. It arises from fear of the ghastly and catastrophic consequences of their use. Thus, in this age which boasts of its atomic power, it no longer makes sense to maintain that war is a fit instrument with which to repair the violation of justice. And yet, unhappily, we often find the law of fear reigning supreme among nations and causing them to spend enormous sums on armaments. Their object is not aggression, so they say – and there is no reason for disbelieving them – but to deter others from aggression. Nevertheless, We are hopeful that, by establishing contact with one another and by a policy of negotiation, nations will come to a better recognition of the natural ties that bind them together as men. We are hopeful, too, that they will come to a fairer realization of one of the cardinal duties deriving from our common nature: namely, that love, not fear, must dominate the relationships between individuals and between nations. It is principally characteristic of love that it draws men together in all sorts of ways, sincerely united in the bonds of mind and matter; and this is a union from which countless blessings can flow (1963, Pacem in Terris*).*

Pacem in Terris was the first papal encyclical to be addressed to all humanity, not just to the Catholic Church. It was the first encyclical to break definitively with 'just war' doctrine as previously outlined in the Western theological tradition. It was also the first encyclical to proclaim that *all* human persons are invested with inalienable rights that are unassailable by any earthly authority. In addition, *Pacem in Terris* shifted for the first time to the fundamental choice of an optimistic perspective of the human person, in stark contrast to the rather negative vision that had previously characterized a very large portion of Western Catholic (cataphatic) theology.

Blessed Paul VI maintained that authentic peace comes only through integral human development, while Saint John Paul II declared that "violence is evil . . . [and] the enemy of justice."

He said, "Violence and arms can never resolve the problems of man . . . violence is a crime against humanity for it destroys the very fabric of society." Pope Benedict XVI stated that violence degrades the dignity of the victim and the perpetrator.

Western Christianity Today on Just War

As has been eloquently elaborated by Pope Francis (2013) and Peter, Cardinal Turkson (2016), the president of the Pontifical Council for Justice and Peace:

"Faith and violence are incompatible . . . [The doctrine of 'just war' has been] used and abused by political leaders . . . it was initially meant to make it difficult to wage war because you needed to justify it. This now has been interpreted these days as a war is just when it is exercised in self-defense . . . or to put off an aggressor or to protect innocent people. In that case, Pope Francis would say: 'You don't stop an aggression by being an aggressor. You don't stop a conflict by inciting another conflict. You don't stop a war by starting another war.' It doesn't stop, we've seen it all around us.

Trying to stop the aggressor in Iraq has not stopped war. Trying to stop the aggressor in Libya has not stopped war. It's not stopped the war in any place. We do not stop war by starting another war. People think that this [nonviolence] is utopian, but Jesus was that. From the point of view of us Christians, and talking as Christians, our master also taught us a way of dealing with violence ['turning the other cheek']. Is it worth following what our master taught us? What he taught s this nonviolence . . . There are several diplomatic means we can use to stop aggression. If nothing else at all, stop that with which people cause the aggression. Why don't you talk about curtailing arms trafficking? The really big instruments of war come from factories and industries which produce weapons and some of these weapons are now in these theatres of war.

The more-than-80 participants in the first-ever Vatican conference convened last year to specifically examine the 'just war' doctrine of Augustine and Thomas explicitly declared in their conclusions:

There is no just war. Too often the 'just war theory' has been used to endorse rather than prevent or limit war. Suggesting that a 'just war' is possible also undermines the moral imperative to develop tools and capacities for nonviolent transformation of conflict. We need a new framework that is consistent with Gospel nonviolence. We propose that the Catholic Church develop and consider shifting to a Just Peace approach based on Gospel nonviolence (2016, An Appeal to the Catholic Church to Re-Commit to the Centrality of Gospel Nonviolence*).*

As Archbishop John Baptist Odama of Gulu, Uganda, said:

['Just war' doctrine] is out of date for our world of today. We have to sound this with a strong voice. Any war is a destruction. There is no justice in destruction . . . It is outdated. The conditions [listed in The Catechism*] are only given to say in reality there should be no war. [Jesus] always asked His followers not to resort to violence in solving problems, including in His last stage of life. On the Cross, He said, 'Father forgive them because they don't know what they're doing.' In this statement, He united the whole of humanity under one Father. He does not take violent words and violent actions. That is the greatest act of teaching as to how we should handle our situations. Not violence.*

Pope Francis

Pope Francis (2016) reiterated that:

The basic premise is that the ultimate and most deeply worthy goal of human beings and of the human community is the abolition of war. In this vein, we recall that the only explicit condemnation issued by the Second Vatican Council was against war, although the Council recognized that, since war has not been eradicated from the human condition, "governments cannot *be denied the right to legitimate defence once every means of peaceful settlement has been exhausted." Another cornerstone is to recognize that "conflict cannot be ignored or concealed. It has to be faced." Of course, the purpose is not to remain trapped within a framework of conflict, thus losing our overall perspective and our sense of the profound unity of reality. Rather, we must accept and tackle conflict so as to resolve it and transform it into a link in that new process which "peacemakers" initiate . . . In our complex and violent world, it is truly a formidable undertaking to work for peace by living the practice of non-violence! Equally daunting is the aim of achieving full disarmament "by reaching people's very souls," building bridges, fighting fear and pursuing open and sincere dialogue. The practice of dialogue is in fact difficult. We must be prepared to forgive and take. We must not assume that the others are wrong. Instead, accepting our differences and remaining true to our positions, we must seek the good of all; and, after having finally found agreement, we must firmly maintain it (*Message on the occasion of the conference on 'Nonviolence and Just Peace'*).*

These past few years, Pope Francis has openly declared that "The world once more is at war and is preparing to go even more forcefully into war . . . the fruit of war is death." This year he further said:

International peace and stability cannot be based on a false sense of security, on the threat of mutual destruction or total annihilation, or on simply maintaining a balance of power. Peace must be built on justice, on integral human development, on respect for fundamental human rights, on the protection of creation, on the participation of all in public life, on trust between peoples, on the support of peaceful institutions, on access to education and health, on dialogue and solidarity. From this perspective, we need to go beyond nuclear deterrence: the international community is called upon to adopt forward-looking strategies to promote the goal of peace and stability and to avoid short-sighted approaches to the problems surrounding national and international security.

In this context, the ultimate goal of the total elimination of nuclear weapons becomes both a challenge and a moral and humanitarian imperative.

A concrete approach should promote a reflection on an ethics of peace and multilateral and cooperative security that goes beyond the fear and isolationism that prevail in many debates today. Achieving a world without nuclear weapons involves a long-term process, based on the awareness that "everything is connected" within the perspective of an integral ecology (cf. Laudato Si, 117, 138). The common destiny of mankind demands the pragmatic strengthening of dialogue and the building and consolidating of mechanisms of trust and cooperation, capable of creating the conditions for a world without nuclear weapons.

Growing interdependence and globalization mean that any response to the threat of nuclear weapons should be collective and concerted, based on mutual trust. This trust can be built only through dialogue that is truly directed to the common good and not to the protection of veiled or particular interests; such dialogue, as far as possible, should include all: nuclear states, countries which do not possess nuclear weapons, the military and private sectors, religious communities, civil societies, and international organizations. And in this endeavour we must avoid those forms of mutual recrimination and polarization which hinder dialogue rather than encourage it. Humanity has the ability to work together in building up our common home; we have the freedom, intelligence and capacity to lead and direct technology, to place limits on our power, and to put all this at the service of another type of progress: one that is more human, social and integral (2017, Message to the United Nations Conference to negotiate a legally binding instrument to prohibit nuclear weapons, leading towards their total elimination*).*

Eastern Christianity Today on Just War

The Patriarch, Bartholomew I, said:

The irrationality of war is evident from its effect on humanity and on the natural environment . . . Through spiritual vigilance and focusing on safeguarding the world from destruction, war and the causes of war must be addressed and eliminated. Peace can only be upheld if the causes of war and hostility in our times are being addressed. Some of the causes of war relate with discrimination, subjugation, hostility, and depressing social conditions. As the causes of war intensify, our chances of upholding peace in the world fade away. For these reasons, we must use all of our resources on a global scale to eliminate these causes. The uncontrollable issues that are the strongest contributors to war deal with nations over-emphasizing preparations for war and increasing the manufacturing initiatives of military ammunition (1999, Address in Athens).

War and violence are never means used by God in order to achieve a result. They are for the most part machinations of the devil used to achieve unlawful ends. We say "for the most part" because, as is well known, in a few specific cases the Church forgives an armed defense against oppression and violence. However, as a rule, peaceful resolution of differences and peaceful cooperation are more pleasing to God and more beneficial to humankind (1999, Address in Novi Sad).

BOOK II

Is Islam a Religion?

Is Islam a Religion or a Sect?

Islam is one of the three monotheistic religions in which the worship of the One, Indivisible God prevails, together with Christianity and Judaism. It is by no means a sect as normally defined, although its various branches (e.g., Sunni, Shia) are sometimes considered to be sects. The God of Abraham, Isaac and Jacob – the God of Jesus Christ (His only-begotten and divine Son), Mary and Joseph – is also the God of Abraham, Hagar and Ishmael. God the Creator is Allah and Allah is God the Creator. Nowhere can this be seen more clearly than in the culture of the Maltese people where the God of Christianity – the God of Catholicism, to be precise – is referred to as *Alla* in the Maltese language.

Muslims worship the same God as Christians and Jews do, even though some, in all three religions, may take intense issue with this fact. Profound misunderstandings and misconceptions abound these days about Islam, especially among more than a few Catholics. Thus, let us see what the Church says about Islam.

The Catholic Church on Islam

From Vatican Council II Onward

"The plan of salvation also includes those who acknowledge the Creator, in the first place among whom are the Muslims: these profess to hold the faith of Abraham, and together with us they adore the one, merciful God, mankind's judge on the last day" – *Lumen Gentium, Dogmatic Constitution on the Church* (1964)

"Then [we refer] to the adorers of God according to the conception of monotheism, the Muslim religion especially, deserving of our admiration for all that is true and good in their worship of God" – *Ecclesiam Suam* (1964).

"The Catholic Church rejects nothing of what is true and holy in these religions. She has a high regard for the manner of life and conduct, the precepts and doctrines which, although differing in many ways from her own teaching, nevertheless often reflect a ray of that truth which enlightens all men. Yet she proclaims and is in duty bound to proclaim without fail, Christ who is 'the way, the truth and the life' (Jn 1:6). In Him, in whom God reconciled all things to Himself (cf. 2 Co 5:18-19), men find the fullness of their religious life. The Church, therefore, urges her sons to enter with prudence and charity into discussion and collaboration with members of other religions. Let Christians, while witnessing to their own faith and way of life, acknowledge, preserve and encourage the spiritual and moral truths found among non-Christians, also their social life and culture.

"The Church has also a high regard for the Muslims. They worship God, who is one, living and subsistent, merciful and almighty, the Creator of heaven and earth (Cf. St. Gregory VII, Letter III, 21 to Anazir [Al-Nasir], King of Mauretania PL, 148.451A.), who has spoken to men. They strive to submit themselves without reserve to the hidden decrees of God, just as Abraham submitted himself to God's plan, to whose faith Muslims eagerly link their own. Although not acknowledging Him as God, they venerate Jesus as a prophet, His Virgin Mother they also honor, and even at times devoutly invoke. Further, they await the day of judgment and the reward of God following the resurrection of the dead. For this reason, they highly esteem an upright life and worship God, especially by way of prayer, alms-deeds and fasting.

"Over the centuries many quarrels and dissensions have arisen between Christians and Muslims. The sacred Council now pleads with all to forget the past, and urges that a sincere effort be made to achieve mutual understanding; for the benefit of all men, let them together preserve and promote peace, liberty, social justice and moral values. Therefore, the Church reproves, as foreign to the mind of Christ, any discrimination against people or any harassment of them on the basis of their race, color, condition in life or religion. Accordingly, following the footsteps of the holy Apostles Peter and Paul, the sacred Council earnestly begs the Christian faithful to 'conduct themselves well among the Gentiles' (1P 2:12) and if possible, as far as depends on them, to be at peace with all men (cf. Rm 12:18), and in that way to be true sons of the Father who is in heaven (cf. Mt 5:45)" – *Nostra Aetate* (1965).

"Faith in God, professed by the spiritual descendants of Abraham – Christians, Muslims and Jews – when it is lived sincerely, when it penetrates life, is a certain foundation of the dignity, brotherhood and freedom of men and a principle of uprightness for moral conduct and life in society. And there is more: as a result of this faith in God the Creator and transcendent, one man finds himself at the summit of creation. He was created, the Bible teaches, 'in the image and likeness of God' (Gn 1:27); for the Qur'an, the sacred book of the Muslims, although man is made of dust, 'God breathed into him his spirit and endowed him with hearing, sight and heart,' that is, intelligence (Surah 32.8).

"For the Muslims, the universe is destined to be subject to man as the representative of God: the Bible affirms that God ordered man to subdue the earth, but also to 'till it and keep it' (Gen. 2:15). As God's creature, man has rights which cannot be violated, but he is equally bound by the law of good and evil which is based on the order established by God. Thanks to this law, man will never submit to any idol. The Christian keeps to the solemn commandment: 'You shall keep no other gods before me' (Ex 20:30). On his side, the Muslim will always say: 'God is the greatest'" – Saint John Paul II. (1979). *Address to the Catholic community of Ankara, Turkey.*

"I deliberately address you as brothers: that is certainly what we are, because we are members of the same human family, whose efforts, whether people realize it or not, tend toward God and the truth that comes from him. But we are especially brothers in God, who created us and whom we are trying to reach, in our own ways, through faith, prayer and worship, through the keeping of his law and through submission to his designs. But are you not, above all, brothers of the Christians of this great country, through the bonds of nationality, history, geography, culture, and hope for a better future, a future that you are building together? Is it not right to think that in the Philippines, the Muslims and the Christians are really traveling on the same ship, for better or for worse, and that in the storms that sweep across the world the safety of each individual depends upon the efforts and cooperation of all?

"I salute all these efforts [of civic and political cooperation] with great satisfaction, and I earnestly encourage their extension. Society cannot bring citizens the happiness that they expect from it unless society itself is built upon dialogue. Dialogue in turn is built upon trust, and trust presupposes not only justice but mercy. Without any doubt, equality and freedom, which are at the foundation of every society, require law and justice. But as I said in a recent letter addressed to the whole Catholic Church, justice by itself is not enough: 'The equality brought by justice is limited to the realms of objective and extrinsic goods, while love and mercy bring it about that people meet one another in that value which is man himself, with the dignity that is proper to him' (Dives in misericordia, encyclical letter 'On the Mercy of God'). Dear Muslims, my brothers: I would like to add that we Christians, just like you, seek the basis and model of mercy in God himself, the God to whom your Book gives the very beautiful name of al-Rahman, while the Bible calls him al-Rahum, the Merciful One" – Saint John Paul II. (1981). *Address to the representatives of Muslims of the Philippines.*

"All true holiness comes from God, who is called 'The Holy One' in the sacred books of the Jews, Christians, and Muslims. Your holy Qur'an calls God 'Al-Quddus,' as in the verse: 'He is God, besides whom there is no other, the Sovereign, the Holy, the (source of) Peace' (Qur'an 59, 23). The prophet Hosea links God's holiness with his forgiving love for mankind, a love which surpasses our ability to comprehend: 'I am God, not man; I am the Holy One in your midst and have no wish to destroy' (Ho 11:9). In the Sermon on the Mount, Jesus teaches his disciples that holiness consists in assuming, in our human way, the qualities of God's own holiness which he has revealed to mankind: 'Be holy, even as your heavenly Father is holy' (Mt 5:48). Thus, the Qur'an calls you to uprightness (al-salah), to conscientious devotion (al-taqwa), to goodness (al-husn), and to virtue (al-birr), which is described as believing in God, giving one's wealth to the needy, freeing captives, being constant in prayer, keeping one's word, and being patient in times of suffering, hardship and violence (Qur'an 2:177). Similarly, St. Paul stresses the love we must show toward all, and the duty to lead a blameless life in the sight of God: 'May the Lord be generous in increasing your love and make you love one another and the whole human race as much as we love you. And may he so confirm your hearts in holiness that you may be blameless in the sight of our God and Father when our Lord Jesus Christ comes with all his saints' (1 Th 3:12-13)" – Saint John Paul II. (1985). *Address on holiness in Christianity and Islam.*

"Christians and Muslims have many things in common, as believers and as human beings. We live in the same world, marked by many signs of hope, but also by multiple signs of anguish. For us, Abraham is a model of faith in God, of submission to his will and of confidence in his goodness. We believe in the same God, the one God, the living God, the God who created the world and brings his creatures to their perfection. God asks that we should listen to His voice. He expects from us obedience to His holy will in a free consent of mind and heart. It is therefore toward this God that my thought goes and that my heart rises. It is of God himself that, above all, I wish to speak with you; of him, because it is in him that we believe, you Muslims and we Catholics. I wish also to speak with you about human values, which have their basis in God, these values which concern the blossoming of our person, as also that of our families and our societies, as well as that of the international community. The mystery of God – is it not the highest reality from which depends the very meaning which man gives to his life? And is it not the first problem that presents itself to a young person, when he reflects upon the mystery of his own existence and on the values which he intends to choose in order to build his growing personality?

"First of all, I invoke the Most High, the all-powerful God who is our Creator. He is the origin of all life, as he is at the source of all that is good, of all that is beautiful, of all that is holy. He made us, us men, and we are from him. His holy law guides our life. It is the light of God which orients our destiny and enlightens our conscience. Yes, God asks that we should listen to his voice. He expects from us obedience to his holy will in a free consent of mind and of heart. That is why we are accountable before him. It is He, God, who is our judge; He who alone is truly just. We know, however, that his mercy is inseparable from His justice. When man returns to Him, repentant and contrite, after having strayed into the disorder of sin and the works of death, God then reveals Himself as the one who pardons and shows mercy. To Him, therefore, our love and our adoration! For His blessing and His mercy, we thank Him, at all times and in all places. Man is a spiritual being. We believers know that we do not live in a closed world. We believe in God. We are worshipers of God. We are seekers of God.

"The Catholic Church regards with respect and recognizes the equality of your religious progress, the richness of your spiritual tradition. I believe that we, Christians and Muslims, must recognize with joy the religious values that we have in common, and give thanks to God for them. Both of us believe in one God, the only God, who is all justice and all mercy; we believe in the importance of prayer, of fasting, of almsgiving, of repentance and of pardon; we believe that God will be a merciful judge to us all at the end of time, and we hope that after the resurrection He will be satisfied with us and we know that we will be satisfied with him. Loyalty demands also that we should recognize and respect our differences. Obviously the most fundamental is the view that we hold onto the person and work of Jesus of Nazareth. You know that, for Christians, Jesus causes them to enter into an intimate knowledge of the mystery of God and into the filial communion by His gifts, so that they recognize Him and proclaim Him Lord and Savior. Those are the important differences which we can accept with humility and respect, in mutual tolerance; this is a mystery about which, I am certain, God will one day enlighten us.

"Christians and Muslims, in general we have badly understood each other, and sometimes, in the past, we have opposed and often exhausted each other in polemics and in wars. I believe that today, God invites us to change our old practices. We must respect each other, and we must stimulate each other in good works on the path of God. With me, you know the reward of spiritual values. Ideologies and slogans cannot satisfy you nor can they solve the problems of your life. Only spiritual and moral values can do it, and they have God at their foundation" – Saint John Paul II. (1985). *Address to the young Muslims of Morocco.*

"Since we are believers in God – who is goodness and perfection – all our activities must reflect the holy and upright nature of the one whom we worship and seek to obey. For this reason, also in the works of mission and da'wah, our action must be founded upon a respect for the inalienable dignity and freedom of the human person created and loved by God. Both Christians and Muslims are called to defend the inviolable right of each individual to freedom of religious belief and practice. There have been in the past, and there continue to be in the present, unfortunate instances of misunderstanding, intolerance and conflict between Christians and Muslims, especially in circumstances where either Muslims or Christians are a minority or are guest workers in a given country. It is our challenge as religious leaders to find ways to overcome such difficulties in a spirit of justice, brotherhood and mutual respect. Hence, by considering the proper means of carrying out mission and da'wah you are dealing with an issue which is important both for religious and for social harmony" – Saint John Paul II. (1990). *Address to the delegation of the World Islamic Call Society.*

"God created human beings, man and woman, and gave to them the world, the earth to cultivate. There is a strict connection between religions, religious faith and culture. Islam is a religion. Christianity is a religion. Islam has become also a culture. Christianity has become also a culture. So it is very important to meet personalities representing Islamic culture. I express my great gratitude for this opportunity and I greet all the eminent scholars gathered here. I am convinced that the future of the world depends on the various cultures and on interreligious dialogue. For it is as St. Thomas Aquinas said: 'Genus humanum arte et ratione vivit.' The life of the human race consists in culture and the future of the human race consists in culture. I thank your university, the biggest centre of Islamic culture. I thank those who are developing Islamic culture and I am grateful for what you are doing to maintain the dialogue with Christian culture. All this I say in the name of the future of our communities, not only of our communities but also of the nations and of the humanity represented in Islam and in Christianity. Thank you very much"-

Saint John Paul II. (2000). *Address to the Grand Sheikh of al-Azhar, Cairo.*

"In a world deeply marked by violence, it is bitterly ironic that even now some of the worst conflicts are between believers who worship the one God, who look to Abraham as a holy patriarch and who seek to follow the Law of Sinai. Each act of violence makes it more urgent for Muslims and Christians everywhere to recognize the things we have in common, to bear witness that we are all creatures of the one merciful God, and to agree once and for all that recourse to violence in the name of religion is completely unacceptable. Especially when religious identity coincides with cultural and ethnic identity it is a solemn duty of believers to ensure that religious sentiment is not used as an excuse for hatred and conflict. Religion is the enemy of exclusion and discrimination; it seeks the good of everyone and therefore ought to be a stimulus for solidarity and harmony between individuals and among peoples" – Saint John Paul II. (2000). *Address to the Ambassador of Egypt.*

"In this context, and precisely here in the land of encounter and dialogue, and before this distinguished audience, I wish to reaffirm the Catholic Church's respect for Islam, for authentic Islam: the Islam that prays, that is concerned for those in need. Recalling the errors of the past, including the most recent past, all believers ought to unite their efforts to ensure that God is never made the hostage of human ambitions. Hatred, fanaticism and terrorism profane the name of God and disfigure the true image of man" – Saint John Paul II. (2001). *Address on culture, art and science, Astana, Kazakhstan.*

"Cameroon is home to thousands of Christians and Muslims, who often live, work and worship in the same neighbourhood. Both believe in one, merciful God who on the last day will judge mankind (cf. Lumen Gentium, 16). Together they bear witness to the fundamental values of family, social responsibility, obedience to God's law and loving concern for the sick and suffering. By patterning their lives on these virtues and teaching them to the young, Christians and Muslims not only show how they foster the full development of the human person, but also how they forge bonds of solidarity with one's neighbours and advance the common good. My friends, I believe a particularly urgent task of religion today is to unveil the vast potential of human reason, which is itself God's gift and which is elevated by revelation and faith. Belief in the one God, far from stunting our capacity to understand ourselves and the world, broadens it. Far from setting us against the world, it commits us to it. We are called to help others see the subtle traces and mysterious presence of God in the world which he has marvellously created and continually sustains with his ineffable and all-embracing love. Although his infinite glory can never be directly grasped by our finite minds in this life, we nonetheless catch glimpses of it in the beauty that surrounds us. When men and women allow the magnificent order of the world and the splendour of human dignity to illumine their minds, they discover that what is "reasonable" extends far beyond what mathematics can calculate, logic can deduce and scientific experimentation can demonstrate; it includes the goodness and innate attractiveness of upright and ethical living made known to us in the very language of creation.

This insight prompts us to seek all that is right and just, to step outside the restricted sphere of our own self-interest and act for the good of others. Genuine religion thus widens the horizon of human understanding and stands at the base of any authentically human culture. It rejects all forms of violence and totalitarianism: not only on principles of faith, but also of right reason. Indeed, religion and reason mutually reinforce one another since religion is purified and structured by reason, and reason's full potential is unleashed by revelation and faith. I therefore encourage you, my dear Muslim friends, to imbue society with the values that emerge from this perspective and elevate human culture, as we work together to build a civilization of love. May the enthusiastic cooperation of Muslims, Catholics and other Christians in Cameroon be a beacon to other African nations of the enormous potential of an interreligious commitment to peace, justice and the common good! With these sentiments, I once again express my gratitude for this auspicious occasion to meet you during my visit to Cameroon. I thank Almighty God for the blessings he has bestowed upon you and your fellow citizens, and I pray that the links that bind Christians and Muslims in their profound reverence for the one God will continue to grow stronger, so that they will reflect more clearly the wisdom of the Almighty, who enlightens the hearts of all mankind" – Pope Benedict XVI. (2009). *Address to the representatives of the Muslim community of Cameroon.*

"I was glad to be able to express my esteem for Muslims and to reiterate the commitment of the Catholic Church to carry forward inter-religious dialogue in a spirit of mutual respect and friendship, bearing joint witness to the firm faith in God that characterizes Christians and Muslims, and striving to know one another better so as to strengthen the bonds of affection between us" – Pope Benedict XVI. (2010). *Excerpt from address to the new ambassador of Turkey.*

"The Synod Fathers highlighted the complexity of the Muslim presence on the African continent. In some countries, good relations exist between Christians and Muslims; in others, the local Christians are merely second-class citizens, and Catholics from abroad, religious and lay, have difficulty obtaining visas and residence permits; in some, there is insufficient distinction between the religious and political spheres, while in others, finally, there is a climate of hostility. I call upon the Church, in every situation, to persist in esteem for Muslims, who "worship God who is one, living and subsistent; merciful and almighty, the creator of heaven and earth, who has also spoken to humanity." If all of us who believe in God desire to promote reconciliation, justice and peace, we must work together to banish every form of discrimination, intolerance and religious fundamentalism. In her social apostolate, the Church does not make religious distinctions. She comes to the help of those in need, be they Christian, Muslim or animist. In this way she bears witness to the love of God, creator of all, and she invites the followers of other religions to demonstrate respect and to practise reciprocity in a spirit of esteem. I ask the whole Church, through patient dialogue with Muslims, to seek juridical and practical recognition of religious freedom, so that every citizen in Africa may enjoy not only the right to choose his religion freely . . . and to engage in worship, but also the right to freedom of conscience. . . Religious freedom is the road to peace" – Pope Benedict XVI. (2011). Post-Synodal Apostolic Exhortation *Africae Munus*.

"The Church's universal nature and vocation require that she engage in dialogue with the members of other religions. In the Middle East this dialogue is based on the spiritual and historical bonds uniting Christians to Jews and Muslims. It is a dialogue which is not primarily dictated by pragmatic political or social considerations, but by underlying theological concerns which have to do with faith. They are grounded in the sacred Scriptures and are clearly defined in the Dogmatic Constitution on the Church Lumen Gentium. . . and in the Declaration on the Church's Relation to Non-Christian Religions . . . Jews, Christians and Muslims alike believe in one God, the Creator of all men and women. May Jews, Christians and Muslims rediscover one of God's desires, that of the unity and harmony of the human family. May Jews, Christians and Muslims find in *other believers* brothers and sisters to be respected and loved, and in this way, beginning in their own lands, give the beautiful witness of serenity and concord between the children of

Abraham. Rather than being exploited in endless conflicts which are unjustifiable for authentic believers, the acknowledgment of one God – if lived with a pure heart – can make a powerful contribution to peace in the region and to respectful coexistence on the part of its peoples.

"The Catholic Church, in fidelity to the teachings of the Second Vatican Council. . . looks with esteem to Muslims, who worship God above all by prayer, almsgiving and fasting, revere Jesus as a prophet while not acknowledging his divinity, and honour Mary, his Virgin Mother. We know that the encounter of Islam and Christianity has often taken the form of doctrinal controversy. Sadly, both sides have used doctrinal differences as a pretext for justifying, in the name of religion, acts of intolerance, discrimination, marginalization and even of persecution . . . Despite this fact, Christians live daily alongside Muslims in the Middle East, where their presence is neither recent nor accidental, but has a long history. As an integral part of the Middle East, Christians have developed over the centuries a type of relationship with their surroundings which can prove instructive. They have let themselves be challenged by Muslim devotion and piety, and have continued, in accordance with their means and to the extent possible, to live by and to promote the values of the Gospel in the surrounding culture. The result has been a particular form of symbiosis. It is proper, then, to acknowledge the contribution made by Jews, Christians and Muslims in the formation of a rich culture proper to the Middle East" – Pope Benedict XVI. (2012). *Ecclesia in Media Oriente.*

"The Catholic Church is aware of the value of promoting friendship and respect among men and women of different religious traditions. We increasingly understand its importance, both because in a certain sense the world has become "smaller" and because the phenomenon of migration increases contact between persons and communities from various traditions, cultures and religions. This reality summons our consciences as

Christians, it is a challenge for understanding the faith and for the concrete life of the local Churches, parishes and so many believers.

"The theme chosen for your meeting, "Members of different religious traditions in society", is therefore particularly relevant. As I stated in the Apostolic Exhortation Evangelii Gaudium, "an attitude of openness in truth and in love must characterize the dialogue with the followers of non-Christian religions, in spite of various obstacles and difficulties, especially forms of fundamentalism on both sides" (n. 250). Indeed, situations in the world where coexistence is difficult are not lacking: often political or economic motives overlap with cultural and religious differences, which also play upon misunderstandings and mistakes of the past: this is all likely to generate suspicion and fear. There is only one road for conquering this fear and it is dialogue and encounter marked by friendship and respect. When we take this path, it is a human one.

"Dialogue does not mean renouncing one's own identity when it goes against another's, nor does it mean compromising Christian faith and morals. To the contrary, "true openness involves remaining steadfast in one's deepest convictions, clear and joyful in one's own identity" (ibid., 251) and therefore open to understanding the religions of another, capable of respectful human relationships, convinced that the encounter with someone different than ourselves can be an occasion of growth in a spirit of fraternity, of enrichment and of witness. This is why interreligious dialogue and evangelization are not mutually exclusive, but rather nourish one another. We do not impose anything, we do not employ any subtle strategies for attracting believers; rather, we bear witness to what we believe and who we are with joy and simplicity. In fact, an encounter wherein each party sets aside his beliefs, pretending to renounce what he holds most dear, would certainly not be an authentic relationship. In this case we could speak of a false fraternity. As disciples of Jesus we have to make every effort to triumph over fear, always ready to take the first step, without becoming discouraged in the face of difficulty and misunderstanding.

"Constructive dialogue between persons of different religious traditions helps also to overcome another fear, which we unfortunately increasingly see in strongly secularized societies: fear directed toward the various religious traditions and toward the religious dimension as such. Religion is looked upon as something useless or even dangerous; Christians are even required at times to act in the exercise of their profession with no reference to their religious and moral convictions (cf. Benedict XVI, Address to the Diplomatic Corps, 10 January 2011). It is widely thought that coexistence is only possible by hiding one's own religious affiliation, by meeting in a kind of neutral space, devoid of references to transcendence. But here, too: how would it be possible to create true relationships, to build a society that is a common home, by imposing that each person set aside what he considers to be an intimate part of his very being? It is impossible to think of fraternity being "born in a laboratory". Of course it is necessary that all things be done while respecting the convictions of others, and of unbelievers, but we must have the courage and patience to come together as we are. The future lies in the respectful coexistence of diversity, not in homologation to a single theoretically neutral way of thought. Throughout history we have seen the tragedy of narrow mindedness. The recognition of the fundamental right of religious freedom in all of its dimensions is unavoidable. The Magisterium of the Church has spoken about this with great commitment in recent decades. We are convinced that world peace passes by this route" – Pope Francis. (2013). *Address to the Plenary Assembly of the Pontifical Council for Interreligious Dialogue.*

The Catechism of the Catholic Church on Islam

The Church's Relationship With Muslims

"The plan of salvation also includes those who acknowledge the Creator, in the first place amongst whom are the Muslims; these profess to hold the faith of Abraham, and together with us they adore the one, merciful God, mankind's judge on the last day.

"The Church's bond with non-Christian religions is in the first place the common origin and end of the human race: All nations form but one community. This is so because all stem from the one stock which God created to people the entire earth, and also because all share a common destiny, namely God. His providence, evident goodness, and saving designs extend to all against the day when the elect are gathered together in the holy city.

"The Catholic Church recognizes in other religions that search, among shadows and images, for the God who is unknown yet near since he gives life and breath and all things and wants all men to be saved. Thus, the Church considers all goodness and truth found in these religions as 'a preparation for the Gospel and given by him who enlightens all men that they may at length have life.' In their religious behavior, however, men also display the limits and errors that disfigure the image of God in them: Very often, deceived by the Evil One, men have become vain in their reasonings, and have exchanged the truth of God for a lie, and served the creature rather than the Creator. Or else, living and dying in this world without God, they are exposed to ultimate despair.

"To reunite all His children, scattered and led astray by sin, the Father willed to call the whole of humanity together into his Son's Church. The Church is the place where humanity must rediscover its unity and salvation. The Church is 'the world reconciled.' She is that bark which 'in the full sail of the Lord's Cross, by the breath of the Holy Spirit, navigates safely in this world.' According to another image dear to the Church Fathers, she is prefigured by Noah's ark, which alone saves from the flood" – CCC, ¶841-845.

Outside the Church There is No Salvation

"How are we to understand this affirmation, often repeated by the Church Fathers? Re-formulated positively, it means that all salvation comes from Christ the Head through the Church which is his Body: Basing itself on Scripture and Tradition, the Council teaches that the Church, a pilgrim now on earth, is necessary for salvation: the one Christ is the mediator and the way of salvation; He is present to us in His Body which is the Church. He Himself explicitly asserted the necessity of faith and Baptism, and thereby affirmed at the same time the necessity of the Church which men enter through Baptism as through a door. Hence, they could not be saved who, knowing that the Catholic Church was founded as necessary by God through Christ, would refuse either to enter it or to remain in it.

"This affirmation is not aimed at those who, through no fault of their own, do not know Christ and His Church: Those who, through no fault of their own, do not know the Gospel of Christ or His Church, but who nevertheless seek God with a sincere heart, and, moved by grace, try in their actions to do His will as they know it through the dictates of their conscience – those too may achieve eternal salvation. Although in ways known to Himself, God can lead those who, through no fault of their own, are ignorant of the Gospel, to that faith without which it is impossible to please Him, the Church still has the obligation and also the sacred right to evangelize all men" – CCC, ¶846-848.

BOOK III

MIGRANTS AND REFUGEES IN CATHOLIC SOCIAL DOCTRINE

Human Persons in Christianity

The new law of love embraces the entire human family and knows no limits, since the proclamation of the salvation wrought by Christ extends to the ends of the earth. *Pontifical Council for Justice and Peace.*[1]

The human person was proclaimed by God the Creator in Sacred Scripture as having been "made in our image, after our likeness" (Gn 1:26; cf 5:1-3; 9:6), so that s/he could live in communion with God the Holy Trinity and one another, while progressing on the path of deification (Saint Irenaeus, *Adv. Haer.*) and becoming a partaker of the divine nature (2 Pt 1:4; Blessed Paul VI, 1965, *Gaudium et Spes*; Saint Athanasius, *De Inc.*; Saint Thomas Aquinas, *Summa Theol.*). The human person is considered to be "the only creature on earth which God willed for itself" (Blessed Paul VI, 1965, *Gaudium et Spes*) and who was given the divine commission:

"Be fertile and multiply; fill the earth and subdue it. Have dominion over the fish of the sea, the birds of the air, and all the living things that crawl on the earth. See, I give you every seed-bearing plant on all the earth and every tree that has seed-bearing fruit on it to be your food; and to all the wild animals, all the birds of the air, and all the living creatures that crawl on the earth, I give all the green plants for food" (Gn 1:28-30).

The human person is thus "not a lost atom in a random universe: he is God's creature, whom God chose to endow with an immortal soul and whom He has always loved" (Pope Benedict XVI, 2009, *Caritas in veritate*). S/he has been granted a dignity and rights that are inviolable by any system in and of the world, because "his sovereignty within the cosmos, his capacity for social existence, and his knowledge and love of the Creator – all are rooted in man's being made in the image of God" (International Theological Commission, 2004, *Communion and stewardship: Human persons created in the image of God*).

The Dignity of the Human Person

Constitutional limits should be set to the powers of government, in order that there may be no encroachment on the rightful freedom of the person and of associations. *Pope Paul VI*.[2]

The inherent dignity of the human person has been described by Saint John Paul II (1988, *Christefideles Laici*) as "manifested in all its radiance when the person's origin and destiny are considered, created by God in His image and likeness as well as redeemed by the most precious Blood of Christ." The Spirit had testified to this in the Old Testament through the psalmist who said, "You are gods, offspring of the Most High, all of you" (Ps 82:6) and "You have made man little less than the angels, you have crowned him with glory and honor" (Ps 8:6). Jesus Christ witnessed to this in the New Testament with the words, "Is it not written in your law, 'I said, "You are gods?"'" (Jn 10:34). God, therefore,

"Who has fatherly concern for everyone, has willed that all men should constitute one family and treat one another in a spirit of brotherhood. For having been created in the image of God, Who 'from one man has created the whole human race and made them live all over the face of the earth' (Acts 17:26). For this reason, love for God and neighbor is the first and greatest commandment . . . [and] love of God cannot be separated from love of neighbor . . . because all men are called to one and the same goal, namely God Himself (Paul VI, 1965)."

In consequence, "every violation of the personal dignity of the human being cries out in vengeance to God and is an offense against the Creator of the individual" (Saint John Paul II, 1988, *Christefideles Laici*). The saint continued,

"In virtue of a personal dignity, the human being is always a value as an individual, and as such demands being considered and treated as a person and never, on the contrary, considered and treated as an object to be used or as a means or as a thing.

"The dignity of the person constitutes the foundation of the equality of all people among themselves . . . All forms of discrimination are totally unacceptable especially those forms which unfortunately continue to divide and degrade the human family: from those based on race or economics to those social and cultural, from political to geographic. Each discrimination constitutes an absolutely intolerable injustice, not so much for the tensions and the conflicts that can be generated in the social sphere, as much as for the dishonor inflicted on the dignity of the person: not only to the dignity of the individual who is the victim of the injustice, but still more to the one who commits the injustice" (ibid.).

Fundamental human rights granted by God. A set of inviolable and fundamental human rights have been thus granted to all human persons by the divine will in virtue of the individual having been created in the image, and after the likeness, of God. These human rights include the right to:
1. Live, from the moment of conception until natural death;
2. Own private property for the shelter of oneself and one's family, within the context of respect for the universal destination of goods;[3] which includes the earth itself;
3. Work for one's integral development and the sustenance of both oneself and one's family, in addition to the right to own the fruits of one's work;
4. Just remuneration for any work done;
5. Rest; and
6. Worship without any undue encumbrances.

[1] In the 2004 *Compendium of the Social Doctrine of the Church*.
[2] In *Dignitatis Humanae*.
[3] This includes the earth itself.

The Social Doctrine of the Church

An irregular legal status cannot allow the migrant to lose his dignity, since he is endowed with inalienable rights, which can neither be violated nor ignored. *Saint John Paul II*.[1]

As part of the aforementioned set of fundamental human rights willed by the divine fiat, the Church has long recognized as part of her social doctrine that the human person has the right to migrate, to sustain his or her own life and that of the family (US Conference of Catholic Bishops, 2017, *Catholic social teaching on immigration and the movement of peoples*).

Pope Pius XII

For example, Pope Pius XII (1952, *Exsul Familia Nazarethana*) spoke with great clarity on this inherent right of the human person as a right that is "founded in the very nature of land." He stated in an earlier letter to the American bishops that:

"You know indeed how preoccupied we have been and with what anxiety we have followed those who have been forced by revolutions in their own countries, or by unemployment or hunger, to leave their homes and live in foreign lands.

"The natural law itself, no less than devotion to humanity, urges that ways of migration be opened to these people. For the Creator of the universe made all good things primarily for the good of all. Since land everywhere offers the possibility of supporting a large number of people, the sovereignty of the State, although it must be respected, cannot be exaggerated to the point that access to this land is, for inadequate or unjustified reasons,

denied to needy and decent people from other nations, provided of course, that the public wealth, considered very carefully, does not forbid this.

"We have condemned severely the ideas of the totalitarian and the imperialistic state, as well as that of exaggerated nationalism. On one hand, in fact they arbitrarily restrict the natural rights of people to migrate or to colonize while on the other hand, they compel entire populations to migrate into other lands, deporting inhabitants against their wills, disgracefully tearing individuals from their families, their homes and their countries."

Saint John XXIII and Blessed Paul VI

Saint John XXIII (1963, *Pacem in Terris*) declared that

"When there are just reasons in favor of it, [the human person] must be permitted to emigrate to other countries and take up residence there. The fact that he is a citizen of a particular State does not deprive him of membership in the human family, nor of citizenship in that universal society, the common worldwide fellowship of man.

"Refugees are persons and all their rights as persons must be recognized. Refugees cannot lose these rights simply because they are deprived of citizenship of their own States. And among man's personal rights we must include his right to enter a country in which he hopes to be able to provide more fittingly for himself and his dependents. It is therefore the duty of State officials to accept such immigrants and – so far as the good of their own community, rightly understood, permits – to further the aims of those who may wish to become members of a new society."

Furthermore, according to *The Catechism of the Catholic Church*, "The more prosperous nations are obliged, to the extent they are able, to welcome the foreigner in search of the security and means of livelihood which he cannot find in his country of origin." No fear of what may or can occur with regard to prevention is valid in terms of the above, despite a country having the right to regulate its borders and control immigration (USCCB,

2017), because this latter right of the nation-State can only occur when carried out with both justice and mercy.

Blessed Paul VI (1963, *Radiomessagio per la 'Giornata della Emigrazione' [Radio message for the Day of Migration]*) declared in a frank manner that migrants often tend to end up suffering from moral and spiritual trauma both peri- and post-translocation, because of the multi-dimensional effects of the migration process itself. He added that it is Jesus Christ who, in fact, is seen "*negli Emigranti è sofferente, è pellegrino, è bisognoso* [in migrants and is suffering, is a pilgrim, is in need]" (*ibid.*).

Saint John Paul II

Speaking within the context of addressing the issue of forced migration due to untenable circumstances in land of origin of the human person, Saint John Paul II (1979, *Messaggio di Sua Santità Giovanni Paulo II a firma del Card. Segretario di Stato Agostino Casaroli per la Giornata Mondiale del Migrante [Message of His Holiness John Paul II as signed by the Cardinal Secretary of State Agostino Casaroli for the World Day of the Migrant]*) stated, "*Faccio appello alla coscienza dell'umanità, perché tutti assumano la loro parte di responsabilità, popoli e governanti, in nome di una solidarietà che oltrepassa le frontiere, le razze, le ideologie . . . ogni uomo, ogni donna, ogni bambino nel bisogno è nostro prossimo* [I appeal to the conscience of humanity, so that everyone assumes their own part of responsibility, peoples and governments, in the name of a solidarity that transcends frontiers, races, and the ideologies . . . every man, every woman, every child in need is our neighbor]."

He (1991, *Migration and religious proselytism: Message of Pope John Paul II to Bishops' Conferences regarding the World Day for Migrants and Refugees*) added that

"Migration always has two aspects, diversity and universality. The former comes from the meeting between diverse individuals and groups of *people and involves inevitable tension, latent rejection and open polemics. The latter is constituted by the harmonious meeting of diverse social subjects who discover themselves in the patrimony that is common to every human being formed as it is by the values of humanity and fraternity. There is a mutual enrichment when diverse cultures come into contact."*

The saint (1991, *Centesimus Annus*) also emphasized the necessity of "abandon[ing] a mentality in which the poor – as individuals and as peoples – are considered a burden as irksome intruders."

In a joint statement the points of which still sound hollowly true today, the Pontifical Council *Cor Unum* and the Pontifical Council for the Pastoral Care of Migrants and Itinerant People (1992, *Refugees: A Challenge to Solidarity*) declared that

"Despite an increased awareness of interdependence among peoples and nations, some States, guided by their own ideologies and particular interests, arbitrarily determine the criteria for the application of international obligations . . . In countries which had in the past offered a generous reception to refugees, there is now a disturbingly similar trend of political decisions aimed at reducing the number of entries and discouraging new requests for asylum . . . respect for the fundamental right of asylum can never be denied when life is seriously threatened in one's homeland."

And speaking about the moral foundation of civil law, Saint John Paul II (1995, *Evangelium Vitae*) stated that,

"[C]ivil law must ensure that all members of society enjoy respect for certain fundamental rights which innately belong to the person, rights which every positive law must recognize and guarantee . . . Thus any government which refused to recognize human rights or acted in violation of them would not only fail in its duty; its decrees would be wholly lacking in binding force."

Speaking about illegal and undocumented migrants, the saint (1996, *Undocumented migrants: Message of Pope John Paul II for World Migration Day*) emphasized that while the issue of illegal migration needs to be addressed at the root level, it is

"necessary to guard against the rise of new forms of racism or xenophobic behavior, which attempt to make these brothers and sisters of ours scapegoats for what may be difficult local situations . . . [it is] necessary to avoid recourse to the use of administrative regulations, meant to restrict the criterion of family membership which result in unjustifiably forcing into an illegal situation people whose right to live with their family cannot be denied by any law."

Placing a particular burden on what this meant in practice for Christians and Catholics in particular, Saint John Paul II continued,

"For Christians, the migrant is not merely an individual to be respected in accordance with the norms established by law, but a person whose presence challenges them and whose needs become an obligation for their responsibility. 'What have you done to your brother?' (cf. Gn 4:9). The answer should not be limited to what is imposed by law, but should be made in the manner of solidarity. Man, particularly if he is weak, defenseless, driven to the margins of society, is a sacrament of Christ's presence (cf. Mt 25:40, 45) . . . Today the illegal migrant comes before us like that 'stranger' in whom Jesus asks to be recognized. To welcome him and to show him solidarity is a duty of hospitality and fidelity to Christian identity itself."

Saint John Paul II (1997, *Message of Pope John Paul II for World Migration Day*) emphasized that

"It is non-Christians, increasingly numerous, who go to countries with a Christian tradition in search of work and better living conditions, and they frequently do so as illegal immigrants and refugees . . . the Church, like the Good Samaritan, feels it her duty to be close to the illegal immigrant and

refugee, contemporary icon of the despoiled traveler, beaten and abandoned on side of the road to Jericho (cf. Lk 10:30) . . . the Christian evangelizes by words and deeds, both the fruit of faith in Christ. Actions, in fact, are his 'active faith,' while words are his 'eloquent faith.' Since there is no evangelization without, in consequence, charitable actions, there is no authentic charity without the spirit of the Gospel: they are two intimately linked aspects."

He (1997, *Message for World Migration Day*) continued,

"For the Christian, acceptance of and solidarity with the stranger are not only a human duty of hospitality, but a precise demand of fidelity itself to Christ's teaching. For the believer, caring for migrants means striving to guarantee a place within the individual Christian community for his brothers and sisters coming from afar, and working so that every human being's personal rights are recognized . . . Jesus' demanding assertion: 'I was a stranger and you welcomed me' (Mt 25:35) retains its power in all circumstances and challenges the conscience of those who intend to follow in his footsteps . . . In this regard, in the words of Saint James, 'What does it profit, my brethren, if a man says he has faith but has not works? Can his faith save him? If a brother or sister is ill-clad and in lack of daily food, and one of you says to them, 'Go in peace, be warmed and filled,' without giving them the things needed for the body, what does it profit? So faith by itself, if it has no works, is dead' (Jas 2:14-17)."

Saint John Paul II (1999, *Message for the 85th World Migration Day*) declared that

"Charity, in its twofold reality as love of God and neighbor, is the summing up of the moral life of the believer. It has in God its source and its goal. 'You shall love your neighbor as yourself' (Lv 19:18). In the Book of Leviticus this commandment occurs in a series of precepts which forbid injustice. One of them warns: 'When a stranger sojourns with you in your land, you shall not do him wrong. The stranger who sojourns with you shall be to you as the native among you, and you shall love him as yourself; for you

were strangers in the land of Egypt: I am the Lord your God' (19:33-44) . . . For the Christian, every human being is a 'neighbor' to be loved. He should not ask himself whom he should love, because to ask who is my neighbor?' is already to set limits and conditions. The reason, 'for you were strangers in the land of Egypt' which constantly accompanies the command to respect and love the migrant, is not only meant to remind the chosen people of their former condition; it also calls their attention to God's action: on his own initiative, he generously delivered them from slavery and freely gave them a land. 'You were a slave and God intervened to set you free; you have seen, then, how God treated migrants; you must treat them in the same way:' this is the implicit thought underlying the precept . . . Catholicity is not only expressed in the fraternal communion of the baptized, but also in the hospitality extended to the stranger, whatever his religious belief, in the rejection of all racial exclusion or discrimination, in the recognition of the personal dignity of every man and woman and, consequently, in the commitment to furthering their inalienable rights."

Speaking in a direct manner about America, Saint John Paul II (1999, *Ecclesia in America*) emphazised with great frankness:

"As for non-Christian religions, the Catholic Church rejects nothing in them which is true and holy. Hence, with regard to other religions Catholics intend to emphasize elements of truth wherever they are to be found, while at the same time firmly bearing witness to the newness of the revelation of Christ, preserved in its fullness by the Church. Consistent with this attitude, they reject as alien to the spirit of Christ any discrimination or persecution directed against persons on the basis of race, color, condition of life or religion. Difference of religion must never be a cause of violence or war. Instead, persons of different beliefs must feel themselves drawn, precisely because of these beliefs, to work together for peace and justice. Muslims, like Christians and Jews, call Abraham their father. Consequently, throughout America these three communities should live in harmony and work together for the common good.

"The Church in America must be a vigilant advocate, defending against any unjust restriction the natural right of individual persons to move

freely within their own nation and from one nation to another. Attention must be called to the rights of migrants and their families and to respect for their human dignity, even in cases of non-legal immigration."

He (2000, *Message of the Holy Father for the World Migration Day 2000*) continued,

"In many regions of the world today people live in tragic situations of instability and uncertainty. It does not come as a surprise that in such contexts the poor and the destitute make plans to escape, to seek a new land that can offer them bread, dignity and peace. This is the migration of the desperate: men and women, often young, who have no alternative than to leave their own country to venture into the unknown. Every day thousands of people take even critical risks in their attempts to escape from a life with no future. Unfortunately, the reality they find in host nations is frequently a source of further disappointment.

"At the same time, States with a relative abundance tend to tighten their borders under pressure from a public opinion disturbed by the inconveniences that accompany the phenomenon of immigration. Society finds itself having to deal with the 'clandestine' men and women in illegal situations, without any rights in a country that refuses to welcome them, victims of organized crime or of unscrupulous entrepreneurs.

"In Jesus, God came seeking human hospitality. This is why he makes the willingness to welcome others in love a characteristic virtue of believers. He chose to be born into a family that found no lodging in Bethlehem (cf. Lk 2: 7) and experienced exile in Egypt (cf. Mt 2: 14). Jesus, who 'had nowhere to lay his head' (Mt 8: 20), asked those he met for hospitality. To Zacchaeus he said: 'I must stay at your house today' (Lk 19: 5). He even compared himself to a foreigner in need of shelter: 'I was a stranger and you welcomed me' (Mt 25: 35). In sending his disciples out on mission, Jesus makes the hospitality they will enjoy an act that concerns him personally: 'He who receives you receives me, and he who receives me receives him who sent me' (Mt 10: 40).

"How can the baptized claim to welcome Christ if they close the door to the foreigner who comes knocking? If anyone has the world's goods

and sees his brother in need, yet closes his heart against him, how does God's love abide in him?' (1 Jn 3: 17) . . . In all the societies of the world the figure of the exile, the refugee, the deportee, the clandestine, the migrant and the 'street people' . . . for believers becomes a call to change their mentality and their life, in accordance with Christ's appeal: 'Repent, and believe in the Gospel' (Mk 1:15). In its highest and most demanding motivation, this call to conversion certainly includes the effective recognition of the rights of migrants: 'It is urgent in their regard that one know how to overcome a strictly nationalistic attitude to create a State which recognizes their right to emigration and encourages their integration . . . It is the duty of all – and especially Christians – to work energetically to establish the universal brotherhood which is the indispensable basis of true justice and a condition for lasting peace' (Paul VI, Octogesima Adveniens*)."*

Saint John Paul II (2001, *Message of the Holy Father for the 87th World Day of Migration 2001*) declared that

"Although it is true that highly developed countries are not always able to assimilate all those who emigrate, nonetheless it should be pointed out that the criterion for determining the level that can be sustained cannot be based solely on protecting their own prosperity, while failing to take into consideration the needs of persons who are tragically forced to ask for hospitality."

He (2002, *Message of the Holy Father John Paul II for the 89th World Day of Migrants and Refugees: For a commitment to overcome all racism, xenophobia and exaggerated nationalism*) added that

"The path to true acceptance of immigrants in their cultural diversity is actually a difficult one, in some cases a real Way of the Cross. *That must not discourage us from pursuing the will of God . . . mixed cultural communities offer unique opportunities to deepen the gift of unity with other Christian Churches and ecclesial communities. Many of them in fact have worked within their own communities and with the Catholic Church to form societies in which the cultures of migrants and their special gifts are sincerely*

appreciated, and in which manifestations of racism, xenophobia and exaggerated nationalism are prophetically opposed."

Furthermore, the saint (2003, *Message of the Holy Father John Paul II for the 90th World Day of Migrants and Refugees: Migration with a view to peace*) stated that,

"No one should be indifferent to the conditions of multitudes of immigrants! They are at the mercy of events, often with dramatic situations behind them. The mass media broadcast moving and sometimes horrifying images of these people. They are children, young people, adults and elderly persons with emaciated faces and sad, lonely eyes. The camps that take them in often impose on them serious restrictions . . . Nor is it possible not to denounce the trafficking practiced by unscrupulous exploiters who abandon at sea, on precarious crafts, people desperately seeking a more certain future. Anyone in critical conditions needs prompt and concrete assistance . . . I deeply hope that every Ecclesial Community, made up of migrants and refugees and those who receive them and drawing inspiration from the sources of grace, will untiringly engage in the construction of peace. May no one let injustice, difficulties or inconvenience be a discouragement!"

[1] In *Message for World Day Migration.*

Pope Benedict XVI

Speaking at length about the difficult situations faced by migrants and refugees, Pope Benedict XVI (2007, *Message of the Holy Father Pope Benedict XVI: 'The migrant family'*) elaborated that

"Shortly after the birth of Jesus, Joseph was forced to leave for Egypt by night, taking the child and his mother with him, in order to flee the persecution of king Herod (cf. Mt 2:13-15). Making a comment on this page of the Gospel, my venerable Predecessor, the Servant of God Pope Pius XII, wrote in 1952: 'The family of Nazareth in exile, Jesus, Mary and Joseph, emigrants and taking refuge in Egypt to escape the fury of an evil king, are

the model, the example and the support of all emigrants and pilgrims of every age and every country, of all refugees of any condition who, compelled by persecution and need, are forced to abandon their homeland, their beloved relatives, their neighbors, their dear friends, and move to a foreign land' (Exsul familia, AAS *44, 1952, 649).

"In this misfortune experienced by the Family of Nazareth, obliged to take refuge in Egypt, we can catch a glimpse of the painful condition in which all migrants live, especially, refugees, exiles, evacuees, internally displaced persons, those who are persecuted. We can take a quick look at the difficulties that every migrant family lives through, the hardships and humiliations, the deprivation and fragility of millions and millions of migrants, refugees and internally displaced people."

He (2008, *Message of the Holy Father Pope Benedict XVI (2009): 'St. Paul, migrant, Apostle of the peoples'*) emphasized the need for the worldwide community of Christians to be more closely conformed to Christ in this respect, because the more a

"community is united to Christ, the more it cares for its neighbor, eschewing judgment, scorn and scandal, and opening itself to reciprocal acceptance (cf. Rm 14:1-3; 15:7). Conformed to Christ, believers feel they are 'brothers' in him, sons of the same Father (Rm 8:14-16; Gal 3:26; 4:6). This treasure of brotherhood makes them 'practice hospitality' (Rm 12:13), which is the firstborn daughter of agape *(cf. 1 Tm 3:2, 5:10; Ti 1:8; Phlm 17).*

"In this manner the Lord's promise: comes true: 'then I will welcome you, and I will be a father to you, and you shall be my sons and daughters' (2 Cor 6:17-18). If we are aware of this, how can we fail to take charge of all those, particularly refugees and displaced people, who are in conditions of difficulty or hardship? How can we fail to meet the needs of those who are de facto *the weakest and most defenseless, marked by precariousness and insecurity, marginalized and often excluded by society? We should give our priority attention to them because, paraphrasing a well-known Pauline text, 'God chose what is foolish in the world to shame the wise, God chose what is weak in the world to shame the strong, God chose what is low and despised*

in the world, even things that are not, to bring to nothing things that are, so that no human being might boast in the presence of God' (1 Cor 1:27)."

Pope Benedict XVI (2009, *Message of the Holy Father Pope Benedict XVI (2010): 'Minor migrants and refugees'*) added that "The migrant is a human person who possesses fundamental, inalienable rights that must be respected by everyone and in every circumstance . . . [remember] the warning of Christ who at the Last Judgment will consider as directed to himself everything that has been done or denied 'to one of the least of these' (cf. Mt 25:40, 45). And how can one fail to consider migrant and refugee minors as also being among the 'least'?" He (2010, *Message of the Holy Father Pope Benedict XVI [2011]: 'One human family'*) continued to elaborate that,

> *"'All peoples are one community and have one origin, because God caused the whole human race to dwell on the face of the earth (cf. Acts 17:26); they also have one final end, God' (Message for World Day of Peace, 2008, 1) . . . Thus, 'We do not live alongside one another purely by chance; all of us are progressing along a common path as men and women, and thus as brothers and sisters' (Message for the World Day of Peace, 2008, 6) . . . All, therefore, belong to one family, migrants and the local populations that welcome them, and all have the same right to enjoy the goods of the earth whose destination is universal, as the social doctrine of the Church teaches. It is here that solidarity and sharing are founded.*
>
> *'In the case of those who are forced to migrate, solidarity is nourished by the 'reserve' of love that is born from considering ourselves a single human family and, for the Catholic faithful, members of the Mystical Body of Christ: in fact we find ourselves depending on each other, all responsible for our brothers and sisters in humanity and, for those who believe, in the faith. As I have already had the opportunity to say, 'Welcoming refugees and giving them hospitality is for everyone an imperative gesture of human solidarity, so that they may not feel isolated because of intolerance and disinterest' (General Audience, 20 June 2007:* Insegnamenti II, 1 *[2007], 1158). This means that those who are forced to leave their homes or their country will be*

helped to find a place where they may live in peace and safety, where they may work and take on the rights and duties that exist in the country that welcomes them, contributing to the common good and without forgetting the religious dimension of life."

Pope Benedict XVI (2011, *Message of the Holy Father Pope Benedict XVI (2012): 'Migration and the new evangelization'*) continued to emphasize that

"Asylum seekers, who fled from persecution, violence and situations that put their life at risk, stand in need of our understanding and welcome, of respect for their human dignity and rights, as well as awareness of their duties. Their suffering pleads with individual states and the international community to adopt attitudes of reciprocal acceptance, overcoming fears and avoiding forms of discrimination, and to make provisions for concrete solidarity also through appropriate structures for hospitality and resettlement programs. All this entails mutual help between the suffering regions and those which, already for years, have accepted a large number of fleeing people, as well as a greater sharing of responsibilities among States.

"The press and the other media have an important role in making known, correctly, objectively and honestly, the situation of those who have been forced to leave their homeland and their loved ones and want to start building a new life. Christian communities are to pay special attention to migrant workers and their families by accompanying them with prayer, solidarity and Christian charity, by enhancing what is reciprocally enriching, as well as by fostering new political, economic and social planning that promotes respect for the dignity of every human person, the safeguarding of the family, access to dignified housing, to work and to welfare."

He (2012, *Message of the Holy Father Pope Benedict XVI (2013): 'Migrations – Pilgrimage of faith and hope'*) elaborated that

"Faith and hope are inseparable in the hearts of many migrants, who deeply desire a better life and not infrequently try to leave behind the 'hopelessness' of an unpromising future. During their journey, many of them

are sustained by the deep trust that God never abandons his children; this certainty makes the pain of their uprooting and separation more tolerable and even gives them the hope of eventually returning to their country of origin. Faith and hope are often among the possessions which emigrants carry with them, knowing that with them, 'we can face our present: the present, even if it is arduous, can be lived and accepted if it leads towards a goal, if we can be sure of this goal, and if this goal is great enough to justify the effort of the journey' (Spe Salvi, *1).*

"It is true that the experience of migration often begins in fear, especially when persecutions and violence are its cause, and in the trauma of having to leave behind family and possessions which had in some way ensured survival. But suffering, great losses and at times a sense of disorientation before an uncertain future do not destroy the dream of being able to build, with hope and courage, a new life in a new country. Indeed, migrants trust that they will encounter acceptance, solidarity and help, that they will meet people who sympathize with the distress and tragedy experienced by others, recognize the values and resources the latter have to offer, and are open to sharing humanly and materially with the needy and disadvantaged. It is important to realize that 'the reality of human solidarity, which is a benefit for us, also imposes a duty' (Caritas in Veritate, *43). Migrants and refugees can experience, along with difficulties, new, welcoming relationships which enable them to enrich their new countries with their professional skills, their social and cultural heritage and, not infrequently, their witness of faith."*

Pope Benedict XVI continued by declaring, "While it is true that migrations often reveal failures and shortcomings on the part of States and the international community, they also point to the aspiration of humanity to enjoy a unity marked by respect for differences, by attitudes of acceptance and hospitality which enable an equitable sharing of the world's goods, and by the protection and the advancement of the dignity and centrality of each human being." The Pope (2014, *Message of the Holy Father Pope Benedict XVI (2015): 'Church without frontiers, Mother to all'*) explained with great clarity that

"In an age of such vast movements of migration, large numbers of people are leaving their homelands, with a suitcase full of fears and desires, to undertake a hopeful and dangerous trip in search of more humane living conditions. Often, however, such migration gives rise to suspicion and hostility, even in ecclesial communities, prior to any knowledge of the migrants' lives or their stories of persecution and destitution. In such cases, suspicion and prejudice conflict with the biblical commandment of welcoming with respect and solidarity the stranger in need.

"Solidarity with migrants and refugees must be accompanied by the courage and creativity necessary to develop, on a worldwide level, a more just and equitable financial and economic order, as well as an increasing commitment to peace, the indispensable condition for all authentic progress."

Pope Francis

The current Vicar of Christ, Pope Francis, in an hermeneutic of continuity with his predecessors, while maintaining an eye on migration as *the* sign of our times, has been no less forthright about the need for Christians and Catholics to open their hearts to the brethren – baptized or non-baptized – who are migrants or refugees. Specifically, he (2013, *Evangelii Gaudium*) said,

"It is essential to draw near to new forms of poverty and vulnerability, in which we are called to recognize the suffering Christ, even if this appears to bring us no tangible and immediate benefits . . . the homeless, the addicted, refugees, indigenous peoples, the elderly who are increasingly isolated and abandoned, and many others. Migrants present a particular challenge . . . I exhort all countries to a generous openness which, rather than fearing the loss of local identity, will prove capable of creating new forms of cultural synthesis. How beautiful are those cities which overcome paralyzing mistrust, integrate those who are different and make this very integration a new factor of development! How attractive are those cities which, even in their architectural design, are full of spaces which connect, relate and favor the recognition of others!

He (2013, *Message of His Holiness Pope Francis for the World Day of Migrants and Refugees (2014): 'Migrants and refugees: Toward a better world'*) continued

"*Migrants and refugees are not pawns on the chessboard of humanity. They are children, women and men who leave or who are forced to leave their homes for various reasons, who share a legitimate desire for knowing and having, but above all for being more. The sheer number of people migrating from one continent to another, or shifting places within their own countries and geographical areas, is striking. Contemporary movements of migration represent the largest movement of individuals, if not of peoples, in history.*

"*We cannot remain silent about the scandal of poverty in its various forms. Violence, exploitation, discrimination, marginalization, restrictive approaches to fundamental freedoms, whether of individuals or of groups: these are some of the chief elements of poverty which need to be overcome. Often these are precisely the elements which mark migratory movements, thus linking migration to poverty. Fleeing from situations of extreme poverty or persecution in the hope of a better future, or simply to save their own lives, millions of persons choose to migrate. Despite their hopes and expectations, they often encounter mistrust, rejection and exclusion, to say nothing of tragedies and disasters which offend their human dignity . . . Working together for a better world requires that countries help one another, in a spirit of willingness and trust, without raising insurmountable barriers.*

"*I would point to yet another element in building a better world, namely, the elimination of prejudices and presuppositions in the approach to migration. Not infrequently, the arrival of migrants, displaced persons, asylum-seekers and refugees gives rise to suspicion and hostility. There is a fear that society will become less secure, that identity and culture will be lost, that competition for jobs will become stiffer and even that criminal activity will increase . . . A change of attitude towards migrants and refugees is needed on the part of everyone, moving away from attitudes of defensiveness and fear, indifference and marginalization – all typical of a throwaway culture – towards attitudes based on a culture of encounter, the only culture capable of building a better, more just and fraternal world.*"

Pope Francis (2015, *Message of His Holiness Pope Francis for the World Day of Migrants and Refugees (2016): 'Migrants and refugees challenge us. The response of the Gospel of mercy'*) added that, "God's fatherly care extends to everyone, like the care of a shepherd for his flock, but it is particularly concerned for the needs of the sheep who are wounded, weary or ill." He continued with even more plainspokenness and forcefulness,

>*"Refugees and people fleeing from their homes challenge individuals and communities, and their traditional ways of life; at times they upset the cultural and social horizons which they encounter. Increasingly, the victims of violence and poverty, leaving their homelands, are exploited by human traffickers during their journey towards the dream of a better future. If they survive the abuses and hardships of the journey, they then have to face latent suspicions and fear. In the end, they frequently encounter a lack of clear and practical policies regulating the acceptance of migrants and providing for short or long-term programs of integration respectful of the rights and duties of all.*
>
>*"Indifference and silence lead to complicity whenever we stand by as people are dying of suffocation, starvation, violence, and shipwreck. Large or small in scale, these are always tragedies, even when a single human life is lost . . . Migrants are our brothers and sisters in search of a better life, far away from poverty, hunger, exploitation and the unjust distribution of the planet's resources which are meant to be equitably shared by all. Don't we all want a better, more decent and prosperous life to share with our loved ones?*
>
>*"How can we ensure that integration will become mutual enrichment, open up positive perspectives to communities, and prevent the danger of discrimination, racism, extreme nationalism or xenophobia? . . . Biblical revelation urges us to welcome the stranger; it tells us that in so doing, we open our doors to God, and that in the faces of others we see the face of Christ himself . . . the voice of Jesus Christ [states] 'Behold, I stand at the door and knock' (Rev 3:20). Yet there continue to be debates about the conditions and limits to be set for the reception of migrants.*
>
>*"Each of us is responsible for his or her neighbor: we are our brothers' and sisters' keepers, wherever they live. Concern for fostering good relationships with others and the ability to overcome prejudice and fear are*

essential ingredients for promoting the culture of encounter, in which we are not only prepared to give, but also to receive from others. Hospitality, in fact, grows from both giving and receiving. It is important to view migrants not only on the basis of their status as regular or irregular, but above all as people whose dignity is to be protected and who are capable of contributing to progress and the general welfare . . . Migrations cannot be reduced merely to their political and legislative aspects, their economic implications and the concrete coexistence of various cultures in one territory. All these complement the defense and promotion of the human person, the culture of encounter, and the unity of peoples, where the Gospel of mercy inspires and encourages ways of renewing and transforming the whole of humanity."

The Pope (2016, *Message of His Holiness Pope Francis for the World Day of Migrants and Refugees (2017): 'Child migrants, the vulnerable and the voiceless'*) elaborated,

"Migration today is not a phenomenon limited to some areas of the planet. It affects all continents and is growing into a tragic situation of global proportions. Not only does this concern those looking for dignified work or better living conditions, but also men and women, the elderly and children, who are forced to leave their homes in the hope of finding safety, peace and security. Children are the first among those to pay the heavy toll of emigration, almost always caused by violence, poverty, environmental conditions, as well as the negative aspects of globalization.

"Among migrants, children constitute the most vulnerable group, because as they face the life ahead of them, they are invisible and voiceless: their precarious situation deprives them of documentation, hiding them from the world's eyes; the absence of adults to accompany them prevents their voices from being raised and heard. In this way, migrant children easily end up at the lowest levels of human degradation, where illegality and violence destroy the future of too many innocents, while the network of child abuse is difficult to break up . . . We need to become aware that the phenomenon of migration is not unrelated to salvation history, but rather a part of that history. One of God's commandments is connected to it: 'You shall not wrong a stranger or oppress him, for you were strangers in the land of Egypt' (Ex 22:21); 'Love

the sojourner therefore; for you were sojourners in the land of Egypt' (Deut 10:19). This phenomenon constitutes a sign of the times, *a sign which speaks of the providential work of God in history and in the human community, with a view to universal communion. While appreciating the issues, and often the suffering and tragedy of migration, as too the difficulties connected with the demands of offering a dignified welcome to these persons, the Church nevertheless encourages us to recognize God's plan. She invites us to do this precisely amidst this phenomenon, with the certainty that no one is a stranger in the Christian community, which embraces 'every nation, tribe, people and tongue' (Rev 7:9). Each person is precious; persons are more important than things, and the worth of an institution is measured by the way it treats the life and dignity of human beings, particularly when they are vulnerable, as in the case of child migrants."*

In a blistering speech given on the occasion of the World Meeting of Popular Movements in February, Pope Francis (2017, *Message of His Holiness Pope Francis on the occasion of the World Meetings of Popular Movements in Modesto, California*) declared with frankness that

"The grave danger is to disown our neighbors. When we do so, we deny their humanity and our own humanity without realizing it; we deny ourselves, and we deny the most important Commandments of Jesus. Herein lies the danger, the dehumanization. But here we also find an opportunity: that the light of the love of neighbor may illuminate the Earth with its stunning brightness like a lightning bolt in the dark; that it may wake us up and let true humanity burst through with authentic resistance, resilience and persistence.

"The question that the lawyer asked Jesus in the Gospel of Luke (10:25-37) echoes in our ears today: 'Who is my neighbor?' Who is that other whom we are to love as we love ourselves? Maybe the questioner expects a comfortable response, in order to carry on with his life: 'My relatives? My compatriots? My co-religionists?' Maybe he wants Jesus to excuse us from the obligation of loving pagans or foreigners who at that time were considered unclean. This man wants a clear rule that allows him to classify others as

neighbor and non-neighbor, as those who can become neighbors and those who cannot become neighbors.

"Jesus responds with a parable which features two figures belonging to the elite of the day and a third figure, considered a foreigner, a pagan and unclean: the Samaritan. On the road from Jerusalem to Jericho, the priest and the Levite come upon a dying man, whom robbers have attacked, stripped, and abandoned. In such situations, the Law of the Lord imposes the duty to offer assistance, but both pass by without stopping. They were in a hurry. However, unlike these elite figures, the Samaritan stopped. Why him? As a Samaritan, he was looked down upon, no one would have counted on him, and in any case, he would have had his own commitments and things to do – yet when he saw the injured man, he did not pass by like the other two who were linked to the Temple, but 'he saw him and had compassion on him' (v. 33). The Samaritan acts with true mercy: he binds up the man's wounds, transports him to an inn, personally takes care of him, and provides for his upkeep. All this teaches us that compassion, love, is not a vague sentiment, but rather means taking care of the other to the point of personally paying for him. It means committing oneself to take all the necessary steps, so as to draw near to the other, to the point of identifying with him: 'You shall love your neighbor as yourself.' This is the Lord's Commandment.

"Jesus teaches us a different path. Do not classify others, in order to see who is a neighbor and who is not. You can become neighbor to whomever you meet in need, and you will do so if you have compassion in your heart. That is to say, if you have that capacity to suffer with someone else. You must become a Samaritan. And then also become like the innkeeper at the end of the parable to whom the Samaritan entrusts the person who is suffering. Who is this innkeeper? It is the Church, the Christian community, people of compassion and solidarity, social organizations. It is us, it is you, to whom the Lord Jesus daily entrusts those who are afflicted in body and spirit, so that we can continue pouring out all of his immeasurable mercy and salvation upon them. Here are the roots of the authentic humanity that resists the dehumanization that wears the livery of indifference, hypocrisy, or intolerance.

"No people is criminal and no religion is terrorist. Christian terrorism does not exist, Jewish terrorism does not exist, and Muslim terrorism does not exist. They do not exist. No people is criminal or drug-

trafficking or violent . . . There are fundamentalist and violent individuals in all peoples and religions – and with intolerant generalizations, they become stronger because they feed on hate and xenophobia. By confronting terror with love, we work for peace. I ask you for meekness and resolve to defend these principles. I ask you not to barter them lightly or apply them superficially. Like Saint Francis of Assisi, let us give everything of ourselves: where there is hatred, let us sow love; where there is injury, let us sow pardon; where there is discord, let us sow unity; where there is error, let us sow truth."

The Vicar of Christ (2017, *The Pope receives the participants in the 6th International Forum on Migration and Peace, 21.02.2017*) elaborated that the moral and social obligations are "to welcome, to protect, to promote and to integrate" migrants and refugees. Pope Francis continued,

"Protecting is not enough. What is required is the promotion of an integral human development of migrants, exiles and refugees. This 'takes place by attending to the inestimable goods of justice, peace, and the care of creation' (Apostolic Letter Humanam Progressionem, *17 August 2016). Development, according to the social doctrine of the Church, is an undeniable right of every human being. As such, it must be guaranteed by ensuring the necessary conditions for its exercise, both in the individual and social context, providing fair access to fundamental goods for all people and offering the possibility of choice and growth.*

*"[There is] a duty of justice. We can no longer sustain unacceptable economic inequality, which prevents us from applying the principle of the universal destination of the earth's goods. We are all called to undertake processes of apportionment which are respectful, responsible and inspired by the precepts of distributive justice. 'We need, then, to find ways by which all may benefit from the fruits of the earth, not only to avoid the widening gap between those who have more and those who must be content with the crumbs, but above all because it is a question of justice, equality and respect for every human being' (*Message for the World Day of Peace, *8 December 2013, 9). One group of individuals cannot control half of the world's resources. We cannot allow for persons and entire peoples to have a right only*

to gather the remaining crumbs . . . This joint responsibility must be interpreted in accord with the principle of subsidiarity, 'which grants freedom to develop the capabilities present at every level of society, while also demanding a greater sense of responsibility for the common good from those who wield greater power' (Laudato Si', *196). Ensuring justice means also reconciling history with our present globalized situation, without perpetuating mindsets which exploit people and places, a consequence of the most cynical use of the market in order to increase the wellbeing of the few . . . For all this there must be redress.*

"There is a duty of civility. Our commitment to migrants, exiles and refugees is an application of those principles and values of welcome and fraternity that constitute a common patrimony of humanity and wisdom which we draw from . . . Today more than ever, it is necessary to affirm the centrality of the human person, without allowing immediate and ancillary circumstances, or even the necessary fulfilment of bureaucratic and administrative requirements, to obscure this essential dignity . . . From the duty of civility is also regained the value of fraternity, which is founded on the innate relational constitution of the human person: 'A lively awareness of our relatedness helps us to look upon and to treat each person as a true sister or brother; without fraternity it is impossible to build a just society and a solid and lasting peace' (Message for the World Day of Peace, *8 December 2013, 1). Fraternity is the most civil way of relating with the reality of another person, which does not threaten us, but engages, reaffirms and enriches our individual identity (cf. Benedict XVI,* Address to Participants in an Interacademic Conference on "The Changing Identity of the Individual", *28 January 2008).*

"There is a duty of solidarity. In the face of tragedies which take the lives of so many migrants and refugees – conflicts, persecutions, forms of abuse, violence, death – expressions of empathy and compassion cannot help but spontaneously well-up. 'Where is your brother?' (Gen 4:9): this question which God asks of man since his origins, involves us, especially today with regard to our brothers and sisters who are migrating: 'This is not a question directed to others; it is a question directed to me, to you, to each of us' (Homily at the "Arena" Sports Camp, Salina Quarter, Lampedusa, *8 July 2013). Solidarity is born precisely from the capacity to*

understand the needs of our brothers and sisters who are in difficulty and to take responsibility for these needs. Upon this, in short, is based the sacred value of hospitality, present in religious traditions. For us Christians, hospitality offered to the weary traveler is offered to Jesus Christ himself, through the newcomer: 'I was a stranger and you welcomed me' (Mt 25:35). The duty of solidarity is to counter the throwaway culture and give greater attention to those who are weakest, poorest and most vulnerable. Thus a change of attitude towards migrants and refugees is needed on the part of everyone" (ibid.).

BOOK IV

IS THE DEATH PENALTY JUST?

You shall not kill (Ex 20:13).

"Cain said to the Lord: My iniquity is greater than that I may deserve pardon. Behold You have cast me out this day from the face of the earth, and I shall be hidden from Your face, and I shall be a vagabond and a fugitive on the earth: everyone, therefore, who finds me shall kill me. And the Lord said to him: No, it shall not be so: Whosoever shall kill Cain, shall be punished sevenfold. And the Lord set a mark upon Cain, so that whoever found him should not kill him" (Gn 4:13-15).

Blessed Paul VI

"Go out into the world and make every effort possible in every way to restore the dignity of man, and all that it implies! I stand foursquare with modern theologians who hold that prudentially and historically capital punishment does not fit into the greater contemporary theological awareness of the worth of each individual on earth" (*Speech to the Bishops at closing of Vatican Council II*, Vatican City, 1965).

Note: Blessed Paul VI removed capital punishment from the fundamental law of Vatican City in 1969.

Saint John Paul II

"On this matter there is a growing tendency, both in the Church and in civil society, to demand that it be applied in a very limited way or even that it be abolished completely. The problem must be viewed in the context of a system of penal justice ever more in line with human dignity and thus, in the end, with God's plan for man and society. The primary purpose of the punishment which society inflicts is "to redress the disorder caused by the offence". Public authority must redress the violation of personal and social

61

rights by imposing on the offender an adequate punishment for the crime, as a condition for the offender to regain the exercise of his or her freedom. In this way authority also fulfils the purpose of defending public order and ensuring people's safety, while at the same time offering the offender an incentive and help to change his or her behaviour and be rehabilitated.

"It is clear that, for these purposes to be achieved, the nature and extent of the punishment must be carefully evaluated and decided upon, and ought not go to the extreme of executing the offender except in cases of absolute necessity: in other words, when it would not be possible otherwise to defend society. Today however, as a result of steady improvements in the organization of the penal system, such cases are very rare, if not practically non-existent. In any event, the principle set forth in the new Catechism of the Catholic Church *remains valid: 'If bloodless means are sufficient to defend human lives against an aggressor and to protect public order and the safety of persons, public authority must limit itself to such means, because they better correspond to the concrete conditions of the common good and are more in conformity to the dignity of the human person'"* (Encyclical, *Evangelium Vitae* ¶56, 1995).

"May Christmas help to strengthen and renew, throughout the world, the consensus concerning the need for urgent and adequate measures to halt the production and sale of arms, to defend human life, to end the death penalty, to free children and adolescents from all forms of exploitation, to restrain the bloodied hand of those responsible for genocide and crimes of war, to give environmental issues, especially after the recent natural catastrophes, the indispensable attention which they deserve for the protection of creation and of human dignity!" (*Christmas Day Message,* Vatican City, December 25, 1998).

"Nowadays, in America as elsewhere in the world, a model of society appears to be emerging in which the powerful predominate, setting aside and even eliminating the powerless: I am thinking here of unborn children, helpless victims of abortion; the elderly and incurably ill, subjected at times to euthanasia; and the many other people relegated to the margins of society by consumerism and materialism. Nor can I fail to mention the unnecessary

recourse to the death penalty when other "bloodless means are sufficient to defend human lives against an aggressor and to protect public order and the safety of persons. Today, given the means at the State's disposal to deal with crime and control those who commit it, without abandoning all hope of their redemption, the cases where it is absolutely necessary to do away with an offender 'are now very rare, even non-existent practically.' This model of society bears the stamp of the culture of death, and is therefore in opposition to the Gospel message. Faced with this distressing reality, the Church community intends to commit itself all the more to the defense of the culture of life.

"In this regard, the Synod Fathers, echoing recent documents of the Church's Magisterium, forcefully restated their unconditional respect for and total dedication to human life from the moment of conception to that of natural death, and their condemnation of evils like abortion and euthanasia. If the teachings of the divine and natural law are to be upheld, it is essential to promote knowledge of the Church's social doctrine and to work so that the values of life and family are recognized and defended in social customs and in State ordinances" (Post-Synodal Apostolic Exhortation, *Ecclesia in America* ¶83, 1999).

"The new evangelization calls for followers of Christ who are unconditionally pro-life: who will proclaim, celebrate and serve the Gospel of life in every situation. A sign of hope is the increasing recognition that the dignity of human life must never be taken away, even in the case of someone who has done great evil. Modern society has the means of protecting itself, without definitively denying criminals the chance to reform. I renew the appeal I made most recently at Christmas for a consensus to end the death penalty, which is both cruel and unnecessary" (*Papal Mass*, St. Louis, MO, USA, January 27, 1999).

"May the death penalty, an unworthy punishment still used in some countries, be abolished throughout the world" (*Papal Mass*, Regina Coeli Prison, Rome, Italy, 2000).

Pope Benedict XVI

"Prisoners are human persons who, despite their crime, deserve to be treated with respect and dignity. They need our care. With this in mind, the Church must provide for pastoral care in prisons, for the material and spiritual welfare of the prisoners. This pastoral activity is a real service that the Church offers to society, and it is one that the state should support for the sake of the common good. Together with the Synod members, I draw the attention of society's leaders to the need to make every effort to eliminate the death penalty and to reform the penal system in a way that ensures respect for the prisoners' human dignity. Pastoral workers have the task of studying and recommending restorative justice *as a means and a process for promoting reconciliation, justice and peace, and the return of victims and offenders to the community"* (Post-Synodal Apostolic Exhortation, *Africae Munus* ¶83, 2011).

"I express my hope that your deliberations will encourage the political and legislative initiatives being promoted in a growing number of countries to eliminate the death penalty and to continue the substantive progress made in conforming penal law both to the human dignity of prisoners and the effective maintenance of public order" (*Papal Address,* Community of Sant'Egidio, Rome, November 30, 2011).

Pope Francis

"It is impossible to imagine that States today fail to employ a means other than capital punishment to protect the lives of other people from the unjust aggressor. St John Paul II condemned the death penalty (cf. Encyclical Letter *Evangelium Vitae,* n. 56), *as does the* Catechism of the Catholic Church (n. 2267) *as well. It can be established, however, that States take life not only through the death penalty and through war, but also when, in order to justify their crimes, public officials take refuge in the shadow of State prerogatives. So-called extra-judicial or extra-legal executions are homicides deliberately committed by certain States and by their agents, often passed off as clashes with criminals or presented as the unintended*

consequences of the reasonable, necessary and proportionate use of force in applying the law. In this way, although among the 60 Countries that sanction the death penalty, 35 have not applied it in the last 10 years, the death penalty is applied illegally and in varying degrees throughout the planet.

"The same extra-judicial executions are performed in a systematic way not only by States in the international community, but also by entities not recognized as such, and they are genuine crimes. There are many well known arguments against the death penalty. The Church has duly highlighted several, such as the possibility of judicial error and the use made by totalitarian and dictatorial regimes who use it as a means of suppressing political dissidence or of persecuting religious and cultural minorities, all victims who, in their respective legislation are termed "delinquents". All Christians and men of good will are thus called today to fight not only for the abolition of the death penalty, whether legal or illegal, and in all its forms, but also in order to improve prison conditions, with respect for the human dignity of the people deprived of their freedom. And I link this to life imprisonment. A short time ago the life sentence was taken out of the Vatican's Criminal Code. A life sentence is just a death penalty in disguise" (*Address to the Delegates of the International Association of Penal Law*, Vatican City, October 23, 2014).

"The Church's Magisterium, based on the Sacred Scripture and the thousand-year experience of the People of God, defends life from conception to natural end, and supports full human dignity inasmuch as it represents the image of God. Human life is sacred as, from its beginning, from the first instant of conception, it is the fruit of God's creating action. States kill when they apply the death penalty, when they send their people to war or when they carry out extrajudicial or summary executions. They can also kill by omission, when they fail to guarantee to their people access to the bare essentials for life. ... On some occasions it is necessary to repel an ongoing assault proportionately to avoid damage caused by the aggressor, and the need to neutralize him could lead to his elimination; this is a case of legitimate defense. However, the presuppositions of personal legitimate defense do not apply at the social level, without risk of misinterpretation. When the death penalty is applied, it is not for a current act of aggression, but rather for an

act committed in the past. It is also applied to persons whose current ability to cause harm is not current, as it has been neutralized — they are already deprived of their liberty.

"Nowadays the death penalty is inadmissible, no matter how serious the crime committed. It is an offence against the inviolability of life and the dignity of the human person, which contradicts God's plan for man and society, and his merciful justice, and impedes the penalty from fulfilling any just objective. It does not render justice to the victims, but rather fosters vengeance. For the rule of law, the death penalty represents a failure, as it obliges the state to kill in the name of justice. … Justice can never be wrought by killing a human being. … With the application of the death penalty, the convict is denied the possibility of to repent or make amends for the harm caused; the possibility of confession, by which a man expresses his inner conversion, and contrition, the gateway to atonement and expiation, to reach an encounter with God's merciful and healing justice. It is furthermore frequently used by totalitarian regimes and groups of fanatics for the extermination of political dissidents, minorities, and any subject labeled as 'dangerous' or who may be perceived as a threat to its power or to the achievement of its ends".

"The death penalty is contrary to the sentiment of humanitas and to divine mercy, which must be the model for human justice . . . There is discussion in some quarters about the method of killing, as if it were possible to find ways of 'getting it right' . . . But there is no humane way of killing another person. On the other hand, life imprisonment entails for the prisoner the impossibility of planning a future of freedom, and may therefore be considered as a sort of covert death penalty, as they deprive detainees not only of their freedom, but also of hope. However, although the penal system can stake a claim to the time of convicted persons, it can never claim their hope" (*Address to the International Commission Against the Death Penalty*, Vatican City, March 20, 2015).

"In a word, if we want security, let us give security; if we want life, let us give life; if we want opportunities, let us provide opportunities. The yardstick we use for others will be the yardstick which time will use for us. The Golden Rule also reminds us of our responsibility to protect and

defend human life at every stage of its development. This conviction has led me, from the beginning of my ministry, to advocate at different levels for the global abolition of the death penalty. I am convinced that this way is the best, since every life is sacred, every human person is endowed with an inalienable dignity, and society can only benefit from the rehabilitation of those convicted of crimes. Recently my brother bishops here in the United States renewed their call for the abolition of the death penalty. Not only do I support them, but I also offer encouragement to all those who are convinced that a just and necessary punishment must never exclude the dimension of hope and the goal of rehabilitation" (*Address to the Joint Session of the US Congress,* Washington, DC, September 24, 2015).

"The commandment 'Do not kill' holds absolute value and applies to both the innocent and the guilty. I propose to all those among them who are Catholic to make a courageous and exemplary gesture: may no execution sentence be carried out in this Holy Year of Mercy" (*Speech after the Angelus,* Vatican City, February 21, 2016).

"The Church not only feels that urgency to assert the right to a natural death, without aggressive treatment and euthanasia, but likewise firmly rejects the death penalty" (Post-Synodal Apostolic Exhortation, *Amoris Laetitia* ¶83, 2016).

"One sign of hope is that public opinion is manifesting a growing opposition to the death penalty, even as a means of legitimate social defence. Indeed, nowadays the death penalty is unacceptable, however grave the crime of the convicted person. It is an offence to the inviolability of life and to the dignity of the human person; it likewise contradicts God's plan for individuals and society, and his merciful justice. Nor is it consonant with any just purpose of punishment. It does not render justice to victims, but instead fosters vengeance. The commandment "Thou shalt not kill" has absolute value and applies both to the innocent and to the guilty.

"The Extraordinary Jubilee of Mercy is an auspicious occasion for promoting worldwide ever more evolved forms of respect for the life and dignity of each person. It must not be forgotten that the inviolable and God-given

right to life also belongs to the criminal. Today I would encourage all to work not only for the abolition of the death penalty, but also for the improvement of prison conditions, so that they fully respect the human dignity of those incarcerated. "Rendering justice" does not mean seeking punishment for its own sake, but ensuring that the basic purpose of all punishment is the rehabilitation of the offender. The question must be dealt with within the larger framework of a system of penal justice open to the possibility of the guilty party's reinsertion in society. There is no fitting punishment without hope! Punishment for its own sake, without room for hope, is a form of torture, not of punishment" (*Message to the 6th World Congress Against the Death Penalty,* Vatican City, June 21, 2016).

"Slavery is a mortal sin; today we say this. Back then, some would say that this could be done because these people did not have a soul!" he said. The *number of people enslaved today is "even more, but at least we know that it is a mortal sin. The same goes for the death penalty; for a time, it was normal. Today, we say that the death penalty is inadmissible"* (*Homily,* Vatican City, May 11, 2017).

"Along these same lines, I would like now to bring up a subject that ought to find in the Catechism of the Catholic Church a more adequate and coherent treatment in the light of these expressed aims. I am speaking of the death penalty. This issue cannot be reduced to a mere résumé of traditional teaching without taking into account not only the doctrine as it has developed in the teaching of recent Popes, but also the change in the awareness of the Christian people which rejects an attitude of complacency before a punishment deeply injurious of human dignity. It must be clearly stated that the death penalty is an inhumane measure that, regardless of how it is carried out, abases human dignity. It is per se contrary to the Gospel, because it entails the willful suppression of a human life that never ceases to be sacred in the eyes of its Creator and of which – ultimately – only God is the true judge and guarantor. No man, "not even a murderer, loses his personal dignity" (*Letter to the President of the International Commission against the Death Penalty, 20 March 2015), because God is a Father who always awaits the return of his children who, knowing that they have made*

mistakes, ask for forgiveness and begin a new life. No one ought to be deprived not only of life, but also of the chance for a moral and existential redemption that in turn can benefit the community.

"In past centuries, when means of defence were scarce and society had yet to develop and mature as it has, recourse to the death penalty appeared to be the logical consequence of the correct application of justice. Sadly, even in the Papal States recourse was had to this extreme and inhumane remedy that ignored the primacy of mercy over justice. Let us take responsibility for the past and recognize that the imposition of the death penalty was dictated by a mentality more legalistic than Christian. Concern for preserving power and material wealth led to an over-estimation of the value of the law and prevented a deeper understanding of the Gospel. Nowadays, however, were we to remain neutral before the new demands of upholding personal dignity, we would be even more guilty.

"Here we are not in any way contradicting past teaching, for the defence of the dignity of human life from the first moment of conception to natural death has been taught by the Church consistently and authoritatively. Yet the harmonious development of doctrine demands that we cease to defend arguments that now appear clearly contrary to the new understanding of Christian truth. Indeed, as Saint Vincent of Lérins pointed out, "Some may say: Shall there be no progress of religion in Christ's Church? Certainly; all possible progress. For who is there, so envious of men, so full of hatred to God, who would seek to forbid it?" (Commonitorium, 23.1; PL 50). *It is necessary, therefore, to reaffirm that no matter how serious the crime that has been committed, the death penalty is inadmissible because it is an attack on the inviolability and the dignity of the person"* (Address for the 25th Anniversary of the Promulgation of the Catechism of the Catholic Church, Vatican City, October 11, 2017).

Revision to the Catechism by Pope Francis

1. The Holy Father Pope Francis, in his Discourse on the occasion of the twenty-fifth anniversary of the publication of the Apostolic Constitution Fidei depositum, by which John Paul II promulgated the Catechism of the Catholic Church, asked that the teaching on the death penalty be reformulated so as to better reflect the development of the doctrine on this point that has taken place in recent times.[1] *This development centers principally on the clearer awareness of the Church for the respect due to every human life. Along this line, John Paul II affirmed: "Not even a murderer loses his personal dignity, and God himself pledges to guarantee this."*[2]

2. *It is in the same light that one should understand the attitude towards the death penalty that is expressed ever more widely in the teaching of pastors and in the sensibility of the people of God. If, in fact, the political and social situation of the past made the death penalty an acceptable means for the protection of the common good, today the increasing understanding that the dignity of a person is not lost even after committing the most serious crimes, the deepened understanding of the significance of penal sanctions applied by the State, and the development of more efficacious detention systems that guarantee the due protection of citizens have given rise to a new awareness that recognizes the inadmissibility of the death penalty and, therefore, calling for its abolition.*

3. *In this development, the teaching of the Encyclical Letter Evangelium vitæ of John Paul II is of great importance. The Holy Father enumerated among the signs of hope for a new culture of life "a growing public opposition to the death penalty, even when such a penalty is seen as a kind of 'legitimate defense' on the part of society. Modern society in fact has the means of effectively suppressing crime by rendering criminals harmless without definitively denying them the chance to reform."*[3] *The teaching of Evangelium vitæ was then included in the editio typica of the Catechism of the Catholic Church. In it, the death penalty is not presented as a proportionate penalty for the gravity of the crime, but it can be justified if it is "the only practicable way to defend the lives of human beings effectively against the aggressor," even if in reality "cases of absolute necessity for suppression of the offender today are very rare, if not practically non-existent" (n. 2267).*

4. *John Paul II also intervened on other occasions against the death penalty, appealing both to respect for the dignity of the person as well as to the means that today's society possesses to defend itself from criminals. Thus,*

in the Christmas Message of 1998, he wished "the world the consensus concerning the need for urgent and adequate measures ... to end the death penalty."[4] The following month in the United States, he repeated, "A sign of hope is the increasing recognition that the dignity of human life must never be taken away, even in the case of someone who has done great evil. Modern society has the means of protecting itself, without definitively denying criminals the chance to reform. I renew the appeal I made most recently at Christmas for a consensus to end the death penalty, which is both cruel and unnecessary."[5]

5. The motivation to be committed to the abolition of the death penalty was continued with the subsequent Pontiffs. Benedict XVI recalled "the attention of society's leaders to the need to make every effort to eliminate the death penalty."[6] He later wished a group of the faithful that "your deliberations will encourage the political and legislative initiatives being promoted in a growing number of countries to eliminate the death penalty and to continue the substantive progress made in conforming penal law both to the human dignity of prisoners and the effective maintenance of public order."[7]

6. In this same prospective, Pope Francis has reaffirmed that "today capital punishment is unacceptable, however serious the condemned's crime may have been."[8] The death penalty, regardless of the means of execution, "entails cruel, inhumane, and degrading treatment."[9] Furthermore, it is to be rejected "due to the defective selectivity of the criminal justice system and in the face of the possibility of judicial error."[10] It is in this light that Pope Francis has asked for a revision of the formulation of the Catechism of the Catholic Church on the death penalty in a manner that affirms that "no matter how serious the crime that has been committed, the death penalty is inadmissible because it is an attack on the inviolability and the dignity of the person."[11]

7. The new revision of number 2267 of the Catechism of the Catholic Church, approved by Pope Francis, situates itself in continuity with the preceding Magisterium while bringing forth a coherent development of Catholic doctrine.[12] The new text, following the footsteps of the teaching of

John Paul II in Evangelium vitæ, affirms that ending the life of a criminal as punishment for a crime is inadmissible because it attacks the dignity of the person, a dignity that is not lost even after having committed the most serious crimes. This conclusion is reached taking into account the new understanding of penal sanctions applied by the modern State, which should be oriented above all to the rehabilitation and social reintegration of the criminal. Finally, given that modern society possesses more efficient detention systems, the death penalty becomes unnecessary as protection for the life of innocent people. Certainly, it remains the duty of public authorities to defend the life of citizens, as has always been taught by the Magisterium and is confirmed by the Catechism of the Catholic Church in numbers 2265 and 2266.

8. All of this shows that the new formulation of number 2267 of the Catechism expresses an authentic development of doctrine that is not in contradiction with the prior teachings of the Magisterium. These teachings, in fact, can be explained in the light of the primary responsibility of the public authority to protect the common good in a social context in which the penal sanctions were understood differently, and had developed in an environment in which it was more difficult to guarantee that the criminal could not repeat his crime.

9. The new revision affirms that the understanding of the inadmissibility of the death penalty grew "in the light of the Gospel."[13] The Gospel, in fact, helps to understand better the order of creation that the Son of God assumed, purified, and brought to fulfillment. It also invites us to the mercy and patience of the Lord that gives to each person the time to convert oneself.

10. The new formulation of number 2267 of the Catechism of the Catholic Church desires to give energy to a movement towards a decisive commitment to favor a mentality that recognizes the dignity of every human life and, in respectful dialogue with civil authorities, to encourage the creation of conditions that allow for the elimination of the death penalty where it is still in effect.

The Sovereign Pontiff Francis, in the Audience granted to the undersigned Secretary of the Congregation for the Doctrine of the Faith on 28 June 2018, has approved the present Letter, adopted in the Ordinary Session of this Congregation on 13 June 2018, and ordered its publication.

BOOK V

WHAT IS THE MAGISTERIUM OF THE CATHOLIC CHURCH?

The Magisterium of the Catholic Church is its authority to establish and teach the genuine and correct tenets of the Catholic Faith. That authority is vested uniquely in the reigning Pope and the bishops in communion with him worldwide. Together with Sacred Scripture and Tradition, the Magisterium is one of the three pillars upon which the Catholic Faith rests and by which it has been and keeps on being transmitted through generations.

Six levels exist to the Magisterium, the teaching authority, of the Catholic Church. The first five of these levels require as a minimum the religious assent of the Catholic faithful. The six levels consist of:
1. Pronouncements of the Pope that are made ex cathedra (extraordinary magisterium);
2. The Bishops in communion with the Pope, defining doctrine at a General Council (extraordinary magisterium);
3. The Bishops in communion with the Pope and together with him, proposing definitely, dispersed, but in agreement (ordinary and universal magisterium);
4. The Pope himself (ordinary magisterium);
5. The Bishops in communion with the Pope (ordinary magisterium); and
6. Theologians (*magisterium cathedrae magistralis*).

According to the declaration of Vatican Council I, all those things are to be believed with divine and Catholic faith which are contained in the Word of God, written or handed down, and which the Church, either by a solemn judgment or by her ordinary and universal teaching magisterium, proposes for belief as having been divinely revealed (*Dei Filius,* Dogmatic Constitution on the Catholic Faith, Chapter III). Not everything contained in the statements of the ordinary magisterium is infallible. However, according to the declaration of Vatican Council II, the Catholic Church holds that infallibility is invested in the statements of its universal ordinary magisterium as follows:

> *Although the individual bishops do not enjoy the prerogative of infallibility, they nevertheless proclaim Christ's doctrine infallibly whenever, even though dispersed through the world, but still maintaining the bond of communion among themselves and with the successor of Peter, and authentically teaching matters of faith and morals, they are in agreement on one position as definitively to be held. This is even more clearly verified when, gathered together in an ecumenical council, they are teachers and judges of faith and morals for the universal Church, whose definitions must be adhered to with the submission of faith* (*Lumen Gentium,* Dogmatic Constitution on the Church, §25).

Such teachings of the ordinary and universal magisterium are not given in a single, specific document. They are teachings upheld as authoritative, generally for a long time, by the body of bishops.

The Magisterium of the Reigning Pope and Papal Indefectibility

The Pope has what is known as his own ordinary magisterium (#4 above), his own teaching authority, and this by divine appointment (Mt 16:18–19). This is separate from, and in addition to, any pronouncements he might make ex cathedra (#1 above).

The Magisterium of the Catholic Church is neither external to the Pope nor separate from him (#1 through #6 above). In fact, for the teaching authority of the bishops throughout the world to be valid and authentic, it necessarily has to be in communion with the Pope.

The Magisterium is neither external to the Pope nor optional with regard to its acceptance and the subjection to it by all the Catholic faithful, because it is the Pope who
1. by divine appointment, has supreme and full authority over the universal Church, including, but not limited, to the Catholic Church itself; and
2. is the Supreme Guarantor, the Supreme Witness, of the Faith by virtue of (a) the charism of truth and (b) the charism of a faith that never fails (Lk 22:32) granted to him, and to him alone, by God as an intrinsic part of the privileges of his office as the Vicar of Christ.

Assistance is given by God to the Pope when the latter exercises his ordinary magisterium: *Divine assistance is also given to the successors of the apostles, teaching in communion with the successor of Peter, and, in a particular way, to the bishop of Rome, pastor of the whole Church, when, without arriving at an infallible definition and without pronouncing in a "definitive manner," they propose in the exercise of the ordinary Magisterium a teaching that leads to better understanding of Revelation in matters of faith and morals. To this ordinary teaching the faithful are to adhere to it with religious assent which, though distinct from the assent of faith, is nonetheless an extension of it* (The Catechism of the Catholic Church, Article IX, paragraph §4:892).

Public statements by the Pope that do not qualify as ordinary and universal magisterium also have an authority that Catholics are not free to dismiss. They are required to give such teachings religious submission in accordance with the declaration of Vatican Council II as follows: *Bishops, teaching in communion with the Roman Pontiff, are to be respected by all as witnesses to divine and Catholic truth. In matters of faith and morals, the bishops speak in the name of Christ and the faithful are to accept their teaching and adhere to it with a religious assent. This religious submission of mind and will must be shown in a special way to the authentic magisterium of the Roman Pontiff, even when he is not speaking ex cathedra; that is, it must be shown in such a way that his supreme magisterium is acknowledged with reverence, the judgments made by him are sincerely adhered to, according to his manifest mind and will. His mind and will in the matter may be known either from the character of the documents, from his frequent repetition of the same doctrine, or from his manner of speaking* (*Lumen Gentium,* Dogmatic Constitution on the Church, §25).

As evidenced in Sacred Scripture, Christ said, *I say to you, "You are Peter and on this Rock I will build My Church, and the gates of Hell shall not prevail against it. And I will give you the keys of the kingdom of Heaven. Whasoever you shall bind upon the earth, it shall be bound also in Heaven, and whatsoever you shall loose upon the earth, it shall be loosed also in Heaven"* (Mt 16:18-19).

Thus, Saint Ambrose said, *Ubi Petrus, ibi Ecclesia, ibi Deus* [Where there is Peter, there is the Church and there is God], because it is Peter – the Pope – who is the Rock, the Guarantor of the Faith, and this by divine appointment. Christ Himself prays to the Almighty Father for the Pope.

Christ, Who is God, declared the true Church to be indefectible. The Pope is, thus, himself indefectible in terms of the Faith and what is needed to be saved precisely because the Church is indefectible. This is true not just when the Pope teaches ex cathedra under the charism of infallibility, but also when he teaches non-infallibly as part of his ordinary magisterium. The Guarantor of the Faith can never fall into the grave sins of apostasy, heresy or schism, because he is safeguarded from doing so by the prevenient grace of God – operating grace (not cooperating grace). Throughout the entire history of the Catholic Church, in which resides the fullness of the Church that was established by Christ while still on earth, no canonically-elected Pope has ever fallen into any one of these three sins or combination thereof while reigning as Pope, despite repeated and apparent claims to the contrary, precisely because of this ongoing gift of prevenient grace. The above-referenced gift of grace, which has been granted to Peter and each one of his successors until the end of all time, is not provided by God for the personal benefit of the Pope. It is provided for the benefit of humanity so that the ark of salvation which is the Church never fails and the gates of Hell do not prevail.

The true Church, therefore, can easily be discerned as being where the Pope is, in accordance with Saint Ambrose's declaration, because it is the Pope and no one else who has been granted the divine gifts of the charism of truth and the charism of a faith that never fails.

Papal Infallibility

According to the declaration of Vatican Council II, the issue of *infallibility with which the Divine Redeemer willed His Church to be endowed in defining doctrine of faith and morals, extends as far as the deposit of Revelation extends, which must be religiously guarded and faithfully expounded. And this is the infallibility which the Roman Pontiff, the head of the college of bishops, enjoys in virtue of his office, when, as the supreme shepherd and teacher of all the faithful, who confirms his brethren in their faith, by a definitive act he proclaims a doctrine of faith or morals. And, therefore, his definitions, of themselves, and not from the consent of the Church, are justly styled irreformable, since they are pronounced with the assistance of the Holy Spirit, promised to him in blessed Peter, and therefore they need no approval of others, nor do they allow an appeal to any other judgment. For then the Roman Pontiff is not pronouncing judgment as a private person, but as the supreme teacher of the universal Church, in whom the charism of infallibility of the Church itself is individually present, he is expounding or defending a doctrine of Catholic faith. The infallibility promised to the Church resides also in the body of Bishops, when that body exercises the supreme magisterium with the successor of Peter. To these definitions the assent of the Church can never be wanting, on account of the* activity of that same Holy Spirit, by which the whole flock of Christ is preserved and progresses in unity of faith.

But when either the Roman Pontiff or the Body of Bishops together with him defines a judgment, they pronounce it in accordance with Revelation itself "which all are obliged to abide by and be in conformity with, that is, the Revelation which as written or orally handed down is transmitted in its entirety through the legitimate succession of bishops and especially in care of the Roman Pontiff himself, and which under the guiding light of the Spirit of truth is religiously preserved and faithfully expounded in the Church. The Roman Pontiff and the bishops, in view of their office and the importance of the matter, by fitting means diligently strive to inquire properly into that revelation and to give apt expression to its contents; but a new public revelation they do not accept as pertaining to the divine deposit of faith" (*Lumen Gentium,* Dogmatic Constitution on the Church, §25).

BOOK VI

THE DIVINE HEART OF GOD THE FATHER IN SCRIPTURE

In Sacred Scripture there exist a total of 28 references, direct or indirect, to the Heart of God the Father (Bovenmars, 1991). Twenty-seven references are in the Old Testament, while one reference is in the New Testament. Many of these references are present in all three major sources of Scripture: that is, (1) the Septuagint; (2) the Masoretic text, and (3) the Latin Vulgate. A few references could be considered doubtful.

The 28 biblical references to the Heart of God the Father are taken from the Douay-Rheims translation of the Latin Vulgate *(The Holy Bible,* 1899/2009) as the Vulgate was derived from the Septuagint, the *Tanakh,* earlier Hebrew texts (including text families), secondary Aramaic sources, and the old Latin texts. The Vulgate is the official canon of Sacred Scripture in the Roman Catholic Church. However, because descriptive language differences exist between the Vulgate, the Septuagint and the *Tanakh,* and the Septuagint is considered the official canon of Sacred Scripture in the Orthodox Church, a side-by-side comparison of the 28 references to the Heart of the Father is provided from both the Septuagint and the *Tanakh* to illustrate the differences.

It should be noted that wherever references are made in Scripture to the bosom of the Father, those are also to be understood as pertaining to the Divine Heart of the Almighty Father. However, those particular references have not been included herewith.

Biblical References to the Heart of God the Father

Below are the 28 references that exist in Sacred Scripture about the Heart of God the Father (Bartolo-Abela, 2012) as found in the Douay-Rheims translation of the Latin Vulgate (*The Holy Bible,* 1899/2009), the Septuagint (Brenton, 2010), and the Masoretic text (Yahwist source; *Tanakh,* 1917/2012).

Latin Vulgate *Douay-Rheims*	Septuagint **LXX**	*Tanakh* **Masoretic**
"It repented him that he had made man on the earth. And being touched inwardly with sorrow of heart, He said: 'I will destroy man, whom I have created'" (Gn 6:6-7).	"And the Lord God, having seen that the wicked actions of men were multiplied upon the earth, and that everyone in his heart was intently brooding over evil continually, then God laid it to heart that he had made man upon the earth, and he pondered it deeply" (Gn 6:6-7).	"And it repented HaShem that he had made man upon the earth, and it grieved Him at His Heart. And HaShem said: 'I will blot out man whom I have created'" (Bereshit-Noach 6:6-7).
"And the Lord smelled a sweet savour and said: 'I will no more curse the earth for the sake of man'" (Gn 8:21).	"The Lord God smelled a smell of sweetness, and the Lord God having considered, said, I will not any more curse the earth, because of the works of men,	"And HaShem smelled the sweet savour; and HaShem said in His heart: 'I will not again curse the ground any more for man's sake; for the imagination of man's heart is evil

	because the imagination of man is intently bent upon evil things from his youth, I will not therefore any more smite all living flesh as I have done" (Gn 8:21).	from his youth; neither will I again smite any more everything living, as I have done'" (Bereshit 8:21).
"And I will set a morsel of bread and strengthen ye your heart, afterwards you shall pass on: for therefore are you come aside to your servant. And they said: 'Do as thou hast spoken'... And the Lord said unto Abraham: 'Why did Sara laugh? saying, "Shall I who am an old woman bear a child indeed?" Is there anything hard to God? According to appointment I will return to thee at this same time, life accompanying, and Sara shall have a	"And I will bring bread, and ye shall eat, and after this ye shall depart on your journey, on account of which refreshment ye have turned aside to your servant. And he said, So do, as thou hast said . . . the Lord said to Abraam, Why is it that Sarrha has laughed in herself, saying, Shall I then indeed bear? but I am grown old. Shall anything be impossible with the Lord? At this	"'And I will fetch a morsel of bread, and stay ye your heart; after that ye shall pass on; forasmuch as ye are come to your servant.' And they said: 'So do, as thou hast said'... And HaShem said unto Abraham: 'Wherefore did Sarah laugh, saying: Shall I of a surety bear a child, who am old? Is anything too hard for HaShem. At the set time I will return unto thee, when the season cometh round, and

son'" (Gn 18:5, 13-14).	time I will return to thee seasonably, and Sarrha shall have a son" (Gn 18:5, 13-14).	Sarah shall have a son'" (Bereshit 18:5, 13-14).
"And the Lord said to him: 'I have heard thy prayer and thy supplication, which thou hast made before me. I have sanctified this house, which thou hast built, to put my name there forever, and my eyes and my heart shall be there always'" (3 Kgs 9:3).	"And the Lord said to him, I have heard the voice of thy prayer, and thy which thou madest before me: I have done for thee according to all thy prayer: I have hallowed this house which thou hast built to put my name there forever, and mine eyes and my heart shall be there always" (3 Kgs 9:3).	"And HaShem said unto him: 'I have heard thy prayer and thy supplication, that thou hast made before Me: I have hallowed this house, which thou hast built, to put My name there for ever; and Mine eyes and My heart shall be there perpetually'" (Neviim-Melachim A 9:3).
"And the Lord said to Jehu: 'Because thou hast diligently executed that which was pleasing in my eyes, and hast done to the house of Ahab according to all that was in my	"The Lord said to Jehu, Because of all thy deeds wherein thou hast acted well in doing that which was right in my eyes, according to all things which	"And HaShem said unto Jehu: 'Because thou hast done well in executing that which is right in Mine eyes, and hast done unto the house of Ahab

heart, thy children shall sit upon the throne of Israel to the fourth generation'" (4 Kgs 10:30).	thou hast done to the house of Achaab as they were in my heart, thy sons to the fourth generation shall sit upon the throne of Israel" (4 Kgs 10:30).	according to all that was in My heart, thy sons of the fourth generation shall sit on the throne of Israel'" (Neviim-Melachim B 10:30).
"What is a man that thou shouldst magnify him? or why dost thou set thy heart upon him?" (Jb 7:17).	"What is man, that thou hast magnified him? or that thou givest heed to him?" (Jb 7:17).	"What is man, that Thou shouldest magnify him, and that Thou shouldest set Thy heart upon him?" (Ketuvim-Eyov 7:17).
"He is wise in heart, and mighty in strength: who hath resisted him, and hath had peace?" (Jb 9:4).	"For he is wise in mind, and mighty, and great: who has hardened himself against him and endured?" (Jb 9:4).	"He is wise in Heart, and mighty in strength, who hath hardened himself against Him and prospered?" (Ketuvim-Eyov 9:4).
"Thou hast quoted me with skin and flesh: thou hast put me together with bones and sinews. Thou hast granted	"And thou didst clothe me with skin and flesh, and frame me with bones and sinews. And thou	"Thou hast clothed me with skin and flesh, and knit me together with bones and sinews. Thou hast

me life and mercy, and thy visitation hath preserved my spirit. Although thou conceal these things in thy heart, yet I know that thou rememberest all things" (Jb 10:11-13).	didst bestow upon me life and mercy, and thy oversight has preserved my spirit. Having these things in thyself, I know that thou canst do all things; for nothing is impossible with thee" (Jb 10:11-13).	granted me life and favour, and Thy providence hath preserved my spirit. Yet these things Thou didst hide in Thy heart; I know that this is with Thee" (Ketuvim-Eyov 10:11-13).
"But the counsel of the Lord standeth for ever: the thoughts of his heart to all generations" (Ps 32:11).	"But the counsel of the Lord endures forever, the thoughts of his heart from generation to generation" (Ps 33:11).	"The counsel of HaShem standeth forever, the thoughts of His Heart to all generations" (Ketuvim-Tehilim 33:11).
"And he chose his servant David, and took him from the flocks of sheep: he brought him from following the ewes great with young. To feed Jacob his servant, and Israel his inheritance. And he fed them in the	"He chose David also his servant, and took him up from the flocks of sheep. He took him from following the ewes great with young, to be the shepherd of Jacob his servant, and	"He chose David also His servant, and took him from the sheepfolds. From following the ewes that give suck He brought him, to be shepherd over Jacob His people, and Israel His

innocence of his heart: and conducted them by the skillfulness of his hands" (Ps 77:70-72).	Israel his inheritance. So he tended them in the innocency of his heart; and guided them by the skillfulness of his hands" (Ps 78:70:72).	inheritance. So he shepherded them according to the integrity of his heart; and lead them by the skilfulness of his hands" (Ketuvim-Tehilim 77:70-72).
"For the day of vengeance is in my heart, the year of my redemption is come" (Is 63:4).	"For the day of recompense has come upon them, and the year of redemption is at hand" (Is 63:4).	"For the day of vengeance that was in My Heart, and My year of redemption are come" (Neviim-Yisheyah 63:4).
"Return, O ye revolting children, saith the Lord: for I am your husband and I will take you, one of a city and two of a kindred, and will bring you into Sion. And I will give you pastors according to my own heart, and they shall feed you with knowledge and doctrine" (Jer 3:14-15).	"Turn, ye children that have revolted, saith the Lord; for I will rule over you: and I will take you one of a city, and two of a family, and I will bring you in to Sion: and I will give you shepherds after my heart, and they shall certainly tend you with knowledge" (Jer 3:14-15).	"Return, O backsliding children, saith HaShem; for I am a lord unto you, and I will take you one of a city, and two of a family, and I will bring you to Zion; and I will give you shepherds according to My heart, who shall feed you with knowledge and understanding"

		(Neviim-Yermiyah 3:14-15).
"Because the children of Juda have done evil in my eyes, saith the Lord. They have set their abominations in the house in which my name is called upon, to pollute it. They have built the high places of Topheth, which is in the valley of the son of Ennom, to burn their sons, and their daughters in the fire, which I commanded not, nor thought on in my heart" (Jer 7:30-31).	"The children of Juda have wrought evil before me, saith the Lord; they have set their abominations in the house on which my name is called, to defile it. And they have built the altar of Tapheth, which is in the valley of the son of Ennom, to burn their sons and their daughters with fire; which I did not command them to do, neither did I design it in my heart" (Jer 7:30-31).	"For the children of Judah have done that which is evil in My sight, saith HaShem; they have set their detestable things in the house whereon My name is called, to defile it. And they have built the high places of Topheth, which is in the valley of the son of Hinnom, to burn their sons and their daughters in the fire; which I commanded not, neither came it into My mind" (Neviim-Yermiyah 7:30-31).
"And they have built the high places of Baalim, to burn their children with fire for a holocaust to Baalim: which I did	"And built high places for Baal, to burn their children in the fire, which things I commanded	"And have built the high places of Baal, to burn their sons in the fire of burnt-offerings unto Baal; which I

not command, nor speak of, neither did it once come into my mind" (Jer 19:5).	not, neither did I design them in my heart" (Jer 19:5).	commanded not, nor spoke it, neither came it into My mind" (Neviim-Yermiyah 19:5).
"The wrath of the Lord shall not return till he execute it, and till he accomplish the thought of his heart; in the latter days you shall understand his counsel" (Jer 23:20).	"The Lord's wrath shall return no more, until he have accomplished it, and until he have established it, according to the purpose of his heart: at the end of the days they shall understand it" (Jer 23:20).	"The anger of HaShem shall not return, until He have executed, and till He have performed the purposes of His heart; in the end of days you shall consider it perfectly" (Neviim-Yermiyah 23:20).
"The Lord will not turn away the wrath of his indignation, till he have executed and performed the thought of his heart; in the latter days you shall understand these things" (Jer 30:24).	"The fierce anger of the Lord shall not return, until he shall execute it, and until he shall establish the purpose of his heart: in the latter days ye shall know these things" (Jer 30:24).	"The fierce anger of HaShem shall not return, until He have executed, and till He have performed the purposes of His heart; in the end of days ye shall consider it" (Neviim-Yermiyah 30:24).

"And they have built the high places of Baal, which are in the valley of the son of Ennom, to consecrate their sons and daughters to Moloch: which I commanded them not, neither entered it into my heart, that they should do this abomination and cause Juda to sin" (Jer 32:35).	"And they built to Baal the altars that are in the valley of the son of Ennom, to offer their sons and their daughters to king Moloch; which things I commanded them not, neither came it into my mind that they should do this abomination, to cause Juda to sin" (Jer 39:35).	"And they built the high places of Baal, which are in the valley of the son of Hinnom, to set apart their sons and daughters unto Molech; which I commanded them not, neither came it into My mind, that they should do this abomination; to cause Judah to sin" (Neviim-Yermiyah 32:35).
"And I shall rejoice over them when I shall do them good: and I will plant them in this land in truth, with my whole heart and with all my soul" (Jer 32:41).	"And I will visit them to do them good, and I will plant them in this land in faithfulness, and with all my heart, and with all my soul" (Jer 39:41).	"Yea, I will rejoice over them to do them good, and I will plant them in this land in truth, with My whole heart and with My whole soul" (Neviim-Yermiyah 32:41).
"Was it not the sacrifice that you offered in the cities of Juda, and in the streets of Jerusalem,	"Did not the Lord remember the incense which ye burned in the cities of Juda, and	"The offering that ye offered in the cities of Judah, and in the streets of Jerusalem, ye and

you and your fathers, your kings and your princes, and the people of the land which the Lord hath remembered, and hath it not entered into his heart?" (Jer 44:21).	in the streets of Jerusalem, ye, and your fathers, and your kings, and your princes, and the people of the land? and came it not into his heart?" (Jer 51:21).	your fathers, your kings and your princes, and the people of the land, did not HaShem remember them, and came it not into His mind?" (Neviim-Yermiyah 44:21).
"For he hath not willingly afflicted, nor cast off the children of men" (Lam 3:33).	"He has not answered in anger from his heart, though he has brought low the children of a man" (Lam 3:33).	"For He doth not afflict willingly, nor grieve the children of men" (Ketuvim-Megilot-Eichah 3:33).
"Son of man, say to the prince of Tyre: Thus saith the Lord: Because thy heart is lifted up and thou hast said: 'I am God, and I sit in the chair of God in the heart of the sea:' whereas thou art a man, and not God and hast set thy heart as if it were the heart of God" (Ez 28:2).	"Thou, son of man, say to the prince of Tyrus, Thus saith the Lord; Because thine heart has been exalted, and thou hast said, I am God, I have inhabited the dwelling of God in the heart of the sea; yet thou art man and not God, though thou hast set thine heart as	"Son of man, say unto the prince of Tyre. Thus said the L-rd God: because thy heart is lifted up, and thou hast said: I am a god, I sit in the seat of G-d, in the heart of the seas, yet thou art man and not G-d, though thou didst set thy heart as the heart of G-d" (Neviim-Yechezchial 28:2).

	the heart of God" (Ez 28:2).	
"How shall I deal with thee, O Ephraim, shall I protect thee, O Israel? how shall I make thee as Adama, shall I set thee as Seboim? my heart is turned within me, my repentance is stirred up. I will not execute the fierceness of my wrath: I will not return to destroy Ephraim: because I am God, and not man: the holy one in the midst of thee, and I will not enter into the city" (Ho 11:8-9).	"How shall I deal with thee, Ephraim? how shall I protect thee, Israel? what shall I do with thee? I will make thee as Adama, and as Seboim; my heart is turned at once, my repentance is powerfully excited. I will not act according to the fury of my wrath, I will not abandon Ephraim to be utterly destroyed: for I am God, and not man; the Holy One within thee: and I will not enter into the city" (Ho 11:8-9).	"How shall I give thee up, Ephraim? How shall I surrender thee, Israel? How shall I make thee as Admah? How shall I set thee as Zeboim? My heart is turned within Me, My compassions are kindled together. I will not execute the fierceness of Mine anger, I will not return to destroy Ephraim, for I am G-d and not man, the Holy One in the midst of thee; and I will not come in fury" (Neviim-Treisar-Hoshea 11:8-9).
"O Lord, for thy servant's sake, according to thy own heart, thou hast shown all this	"And thou hast wrought all this greatness according to thine	"O HaShem, for Thy servant's sake, and according to Thine own heart, hast Thou

magnificence, and wouldst have all the great things to be known" (1 Chr 17:19).	heart" (1 Chr 17:19).	wrought all this greatness, to make known all these great things" (Ketuvim-Megilot-Divrei Yamim A 17:19).
"For I have chosen and have sanctified this place, that my name may be there forever, and my eyes and my heart may remain there perpetually" (2 Chr 7:16).	"Now I have chosen and sanctified this house, that my name should be there forever: and my eyes and my heart shall be there always" (2 Chr 7:16).	"Now have I chosen and hallowed this house, that My name may be there forever; and Mine eyes and My heart shall be there perpetually" (Ketuvim-Megilot-Divrei Yamim B 7:15-16).
"And I shall raise me up a faithful priest, who shall do according to my heart, and my soul, and I will build him a faithful house, and he shall walk all days before my anointed" (1 Kgs 2:35).	"I will raise up to myself a faithful priest, who shall do all that is in my heart and in my soul; and I will build him a sure house, and he shall walk before my Christ forever" (1 Kgs 2:35).	"I will raise Me up a faithful priest, that shall do according to that which is in My heart and in My mind; and I will build him a sure house, and he shall walk before Mine anointed forever" (Neviim-Shmuel A 2:35).

"But thy kingdom shall not continue. The Lord hath sought him a man according to his own heart: and him hath the Lord commanded to be prince over his people, because thou hast not observed that which the Lord commanded" (1 Kgs 13:14).	"Now thy kingdom shall not stand to thee, and the Lord shall seek for himself a man after his own heart; and the Lord shall appoint him to be a ruler over his people, because thou hast not kept all that the Lord commanded thee" (1 Kgs 13:14).	"But now thy kingdom shall not continue; HaShem hath sought Him a man after His own heart, and HaShem hath appointed him to be prince over His people, because thou hast not kept that which HaShem commanded thee" (Neviim-Shmuel A 13:14).
"For thy word's sake and according to thy own heart thou hast done all these great things, so that thou wouldst make it known to thy servant" (2 Kgs 7:21).	"And thou hast wrought for thy servant's sake, and according to thy heart thou hast wrought all this greatness, to make it known to thy servant" (2 Kgs 7:21).	"For Thy words sake, and according to Thine own heart, hast Thou wrought all this greatness, to make Thy servant know it" (Neviim-Shmuel B 7:20-21).
"And when he had removed him, he raised them up David to be king, to whom giving testimony, he said: 'I have found David,	"Now thy kingdom shall not stand to thee, and the Lord shall seek for himself a man after his own heart; and the	"But now thy kingdom shall not continue; HaShem hath sought Him a man after His own heart, and HaShem hath

the son of Jesse, a man according to my own heart, who shall do all my wills" (Acts 13:22).	Lord shall appoint him to be a ruler over his people, because thou hast not kept all that the Lord commanded thee" (1 Kgs 13:14).	appointed him to be prince over His people, because thou hast not kept that which HaShem commanded thee" (Neviim-Shmuel A 13:14).

References

Bartolo-Abela, M. (2012). *The icon of the Divine Heart of God the Father: Apologia and canon.* East Longmeadow, MA: Apostolate of the Divine Heart.

Bovenmars, J. G. (1991). *Biblical spirituality of the heart.* NY: Alba House.

Brenton, L. (2010). *English translation of the Greek Septuagint, including the Apocrypha* (Kindle ed.).

The Holy Bible: Douay-Rheims version. (1899/2009). Charlotte, NC: St. Benedict Press.

The Tanakh. (1917/2012). NY: Jewish Publication Society. Retrieved on January 4, 2012 from: http://www.jewishvirtuallibrary.org/ jsource/Bible/jpstoc.html

THE END